# SMART DOLPHIN ZONE

## two 2

### English for Elementary

*by Patricia Avila*

# DATOS EDITORIALES

**Published by UnilX Education**
books@unilxeducation.com
USA +1 619 798 6274
MEX +52 6631030487

MyEnglishGameZone®, 2021 ©UnilX LLC, 2021

All rights reserved. No part of this publication may be reproduced, stored in a retrieval system, or transmitted in any form or by any means, electronic, mechanical, photocopying, recording, or otherwise, without the prior permission of the copyright owner.

First Published 2021

Author: Patricia Armida Ávila Delfín
Main Characters: My English Game Zone®
Cover and Complimentary Graphics: UnilX, Innovalingua Design Team and Freepik.com
Illustration, Design and Animation Leader: Rafael Orellana
Proofreader: Sandra Rojas
Editorial Design: UNIGRÁPHICA
      Rogelio Núñez Osuna
      José Chairez Parda
      Siham Núñez Osuna
      Julieta García García

# PROGRAM SYNOPSIS

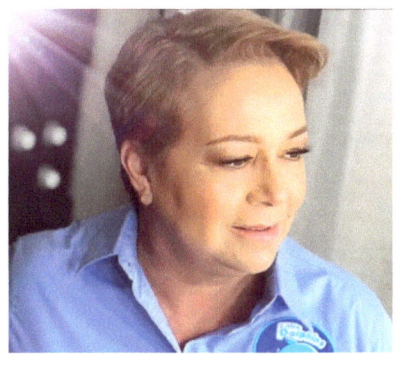

The fundamental objective of Smart Dolphin Zone is learning to communicate through interaction in the target language. The Theory of Language learning tells us that "language is a tool for communication and that students learn a language by using it to communicate."

You will find that Smart Dolphin Zone is a series based on guided everyday communicative interaction. E.g. when students are faced with real life dialogs to find out the schedule of the week's exams or to describe a classmate by his/her physical appearance, among many other authentic situations. Guided dialogs provide opportunities for language learners to interact with each other or with native speakers while feeling comfortable doing so.

This series also acknowledges the role of grammar as that of great importance for our learners to reach higher levels of proficiency and introduces the basic structures from the start of the program.

Smart Dolphin Zone also makes extensive use of authentic texts like: songs, jokes, rhymes, tongue twisters and popular children's stories. They will enrich the knowledge of culture through language.

As you can see, Smart Dolphin Zone has a solid base on the most important methodologies necessary to enhance the learning of the second language in a **dynamic** and **fun** way.

*Patricia Avila Delfín*

# METHODOLOGIES

### Vocabulary Learning

*Vocabulary learning* is central to language acquisition.

Specialists emphasize the need for a systematic and principled approach of vocabulary by the teacher and the learner. Teaching techniques and activities state that new words should not be learned by simple rote memorization.

It is important that new vocabulary items be presented in contexts rich enough to provide clues to meaning and that students be given multiple exposure to items they should learn.

### Communicative Language Learning

Learning to communicate through interaction in the target language is the principal characteristic of the *Communicative Language Teaching* approach.

The *Theory of Language Learning* states that:
• Language is a tool for communication
• Students learn a language by using it to communicate

### Integrated Skills Approach

The four basic skills in language teaching are: listening, speaking, reading, writing.

When we acquire a second language in a natural way the skills appear in that same order.

But why should we integrate the four skills when teaching the second language? If we are focused on teaching a realistic communication competence, the four skills must be developed in an integrated way.

Integrating the skills allows us to use more variety in the lessons because the range of activities will be ampler.

### Spiral Learning

Learning should work like a game in a spiral, that gets a child interested while repeating and gradually increasing difficulty. It also gives students challenging activities and at the same time adds new skills.

The steps to achieve Spiral Learning are:
- Introduce new language. Move forward.
- Recap the important language learned so far.
- Add more language.
- Recap selected language: recent and earlier.
- Repeat the process.

### Topic Based Approach

Topic based approach is student-centered. It helps with students' attention span.

It will hold students' interest from the start to the end of the lesson.

# COURSE STRUCTURE

| Book number | CEFR | LEVELS (12) | NUMBER OF UNITS (180) | NUMBER OF LESSONS (900) |
|---|---|---|---|---|
| 1 | Pre- A1 | 1<br>2 | 15<br>15 | 75<br>75 |
| 2 | A1.1<br>A1.2 | 3<br>4 | 15<br>15 | 75<br>75 |
| 3 | A2.1 | 5<br>6 | 15<br>15 | 75<br>75 |
| 4 | A2.2 | 7<br>8 | 15<br>15 | 75<br>75 |
| 5 | B1.1<br>B1.2 | 9<br>10 | 15<br>15 | 75<br>75 |
| 6 | B1.3<br>B1+ | 11<br>12 | 15<br>15 | 75<br>75 |

# SERIES FEATURES

- Each book with 30 units.
- Two different levels in each book.
- Each unit has five lessons:

**Lesson 1: Vocabulary**
In this first lesson the vocabulary that will be used during the rest of the unit will be presented through clear images that represent each word.

**Lesson 2: Dialogs**
The dialogs will recap the vocabulary items from lesson one and use them in everyday real situations.

**Lesson 3: Reading**
The reading texts will go from original stories that take the ideas of the dialogs and complete them in a text to popular stories from children's literature.

**Lesson 4: Writing**
Prompted writing is used in the lower levels. It encourages students to use their imagination to come up with new and creative ideas for the text. In the higher levels, students will be asked to arrange the paragraphs or the missing sentences to complete the stories they read before.

**Lesson 5: Language in Use**
The last part of each unit, recaps the grammar structures seen, through the presentation of language in use of the four lessons before it. There are activities that will evaluate the knowledge acquired.

# CONTENTS MAP

| LEVEL CEFR | UNIT | TOPIC | VOCABULARY | LANGUAGE IN USE | CAN DO STATEMENT |
|---|---|---|---|---|---|
| 3 A1.1 | 1 | Let's play around the world! | Alphabet Countries Numbers | BE Present Simple Affirmative Interrogative Negative | I can understand questions about myself. I can count to 20. |
| | 2 | Let's play at home! | Family Rooms at Home | Present Progressive Affirmative Interrogative Negative | I can understand simple phrases and sentences concerning my family. |
| | 3 | Let's play with animals! | Animals, Zoo, Farm, Home | Present Simple Affirmative Negative Interrogative | I can tell the names of all the animals I know. I can talk about animals in short sentences. |
| | 4 | Let's celebrate! | Holidays Time Expressions | Future-BE+ Going To Affirmative ** Time To Rhyme: "Hey Diddle Diddle!" | I can say when the main festivals are in the year. I can recite some rhymes. |
| | 5 | Let's play with food! | Food, Breakfast, Lunch, Dinner, Drinks | Future- BE+ Going To Interrogative | I can ask for food and drinks and say thank you. |
| | 6 | Let's play at school! | School Bag Articles | Future- BE+ Going To Negative | I can ask for things in the classroom. |
| | 7 | Let's play with countries! | Countries, City, Beach, Mountain | Future- BE + Going To Wh-Questions | I can talk about my vacation using simple and short sentences. |
| | 8 | Let's play after school! | After School Activities School Subjects | Can-Can't **Time To Rhyme: "Now I Lay Me" | I can ask and answer simple short questions about free time activities |
| | 9 | Let's play with the weather! | Weather /Clothes | Have To Has To Interrogative | I can talk about the seasons in simple short sentences |
| | 10 | Let's play with the seasons! | Clothes | Have To Has To Negative | I can say the words for the seasons and for the weather in different seasons |
| | 11 | Let's play with magic words! | Magic Words | Capital Letters In Days And Months | I can ask for and can give things I can borrow school material |
| | 12 | Let's play around the city! | City Buildings Prepositions | Imperatives Prepositions ** Time To Rhyme "Wee Willie Winkie" | I can ask for directions and give directions in simple short sentences. I can recite some rhymes. |
| | 13 | Let's play with toys! | Toys | Possessive Pronouns Future- BE + Going To Affirmative, Negative Interrogative | I can name common objects. |
| | 14 | Let's play with food! | Food | Future-BE + Going To Wh-Questions | I can name some foods and drinks. |
| | 15 | Let's play! | Games | Future – BE +Going To Wh Questions | I can ask someone to play a game. |

# CONTENTS MAP

| LEVEL CEFR | UNIT | TOPIC | VOCABULARY | LANGUAGE IN USE | CAN DO STATEMENT |
|---|---|---|---|---|---|
| 4 A1.2 | 1 / 16 | Let's play with feelings! | Feelings | Future- Will Affirmative | I can talk about how I feel in simple short sentences. |
| | 2 / 17 | Let's play with time! | Time Expressions | Future- Will Interrogative **Time To Rhyme! "A Wise Old Owl" | I can answer simple questions about what I do on different days. I can recite some rhymes I like. |
| | 3 / 18 | Let's play with transportation! | Transportation | Future-Will Negative | I can indicate the month, day, and time. I can describe vehicles and means of transportation in simple, short sentences |
| | 4 / 19 | Let's play with the weather! | Weather Clothes | Future-Will Short Answers | I can say the words for the weather in different seasons. I can say what the weather is like. |
| | 5 / 20 | Let's play after school! | After School Activities | Future- Will Wh- Questions ** Time To Rhyme! "What Are Little Girls Made Of?" | I can ask questions about vacations. I can recite some rhymes I like. |
| | 6 / 21 | Let's play with school supplies! | School Supplies | Possessive Form Of Nouns | I can say a few sentences words and short phrases naming classroom objects. I can describe my school things in simple, short sentences, |
| | 7 / 22 | Let's play with illnesses! | Illnesses | Illnesses Sympathy Expressions | I can ask somebody about how they are I can ask how someone is, and say how I am. |
| | 8 / 23 | Let's play with irregular plurals! | Irregular Plurals | Irregular Plurals | I can ask simple questions and fixed expressions. |
| | 9 / 24 | Let's play at home! | Home Furniture | Order Of Adjectives There Is-Are | I can use simple sentences to describe my house. |
| | 10 / 25 | Let's play in our free time! | Free Time Activities | Object pronouns | I can ask someone what they like or don't like. I can understand when someone speaks about free time activities. |
| | 11 / 26 | Let's play with numbers! | Numbers 1-100 | Plural Form Of Nouns | I can use numbers, quantity, prices and time. |
| | 12 / 27 | Let's play with opposites! | Adjectives Physical Appearance And Personality Community Helpers | Adjectives To Describe Physical Appearance And Personality | I can find opposites in people. I can speak in simple sentences about people I know. |
| | 13 / 28 | Let's play with time! | Time Expressions | Time Expressions | I can make simple short statements about the lesson plan. |
| | 14 / 29 | Let's play with the days! | Days Of The Week | Future- BE + Going To Affirmative, Negative, Interrogative, Wh- Questions | I can answer simple questions about what I do on different days. |
| | 15 / 30 | Let's play with the months of the year! | Months Of The Year | Future- Will Affirmative, Negative Interrogative, Wh- Questions | I can understand when someone talks about his/ her holidays using simple short sentences. |

**Level THREE Unit ONE**
Let's play around the world!

## Learn the countries

USA    England    France    Japan    Mexico

| 1 one | 2 two | 3 three | 4 four | 5 five |
|---|---|---|---|---|
| 6 six | 7 seven | 8 eight | 9 nine | 10 ten |
| 11 eleven | 12 twelve | 13 thirteen | 14 fourteen | 15 fifteen |
| 16 sixteen | 17 seventeen | 18 eighteen | 19 nineteen | 20 twenty |

| Aa | Bb | Cc | Dd | Ee |
|---|---|---|---|---|
| Ff | Gg | Hh | Ii | Jj |
| Kk | Ll | Mm | Nn | Oo |
| Pp | Qq | Rr | Ss | Tt |
| Uu | Vv | Ww | Xx | Yy |
| Zz | | | | |

**1.2 Dialogs**

Level THREE Unit ONE
Let's play around the world!

## Practice the dialogs

Good morning!
What's your name?
-My name is Michelle.
How do you spell it?
-M-I-C-H-E-L-L-E
How old are you?
-I'm 7 years old.
Where are you from?
-I'm from France.

Good morning!
What's your name?
-My name is Akiko.
How do you spell it?
-A-K-I-K-O
How old are you?
-I'm 7 years old.
Where are you from?
-I'm from Japan.

Good morning!
What's your name?
-My name is Harry.
How do you spell it?
-H-A-R-R-Y
How old are you?
-I'm 8 years old.
Where are you from?
-I'm from England.

Good morning!
What's your name?
-My name is Tom.
How do you spell it?
-T-O-M
How old are you?
-I'm 8 years old.
Where are you from?
-I'm from the USA.

Good morning!
What's your name?
-My name is Rosa.
How do you spell it?
-R-O-S-A
How old are you?
-I'm 8 years old.
Where are you from?
-I'm from Mexico.

Good morning!
What's your name?
-My name is _____.
How do you spell it?
-___ ___ ___ ___ ___ ___ ___
How old are you?
-I'm _____ years old.
Where are you from?
-I'm from _____.

Now you!

**Level THREE Unit ONE**
Let's play around the world!

1.3 Reading

## New friends

There are new friends at school.
They are Michelle, Akiko, Harry and Tom.
Michelle is 7 years old; she isn't from England, she's from France.
Akiko is 7 years old; she isn't from the USA, she's from Japan.
Harry is 8 years old; he isn't from France, he's from England.
Tom is 8 years old; he isn't from Japan, he's from the USA.
Welcome to our school new friends!

### Where are they from?

1. Where is Tom from?
   ❏ France   ❏ USA   ❏ Japan

2. Where is Akiko from?
   ❏ France   ❏ USA   ❏ Japan

3. Where is Harry from?
   ❏ England   ❏ France   ❏ USA

4. Where is Michelle from?
   ❏ England   ❏ Japan   ❏ France

### Read the sentences and circle true or false

1. Tom is seven years old.
   True     False

2. Akiko is from France.
   True     False

3. Harry is from England.
   True     False

4. Michelle is from Japan.
   True     False

5. Tom is from England.
   True     False

11

**1.4 Writing**

Level THREE Unit ONE
Let's play around the world!

Complete the reading with the words from the box below in any order and times you think necessary.

### New friends

There are new friends at school.
They are Michelle, Akiko, Harry and Tom.
Michelle is _____ years old; she isn't from _____,
she's from _____.
Akiko is _____ years old; she isn't from _____,
she's from _____.
Harry is _____ years old; he isn't from _____,
he's from _____.
Tom is _____ years old; he isn't from _____,
he's from _____.
Welcome to our school new friends!

5 • 6 • 7 • 8 • 9 • 10
France • the USA • Japan • England

**Level THREE Unit ONE**
Let's play around the world!

1.5 Language in use

**Present Simple Tense verb BE**
We use the verb BE in the Present Simple to talk about names, professions, nationalities, age and feelings

Affirmative form:
I am
He/she/it is
We/you/they are

Negative form:
I am+not
He/she/it is + not
We/you/they are + not

Interrogative form:
Am I?
Is he/she/it?
Are you/they/we?

## Unscramble the sentences

1. ___ ___ ___ ___ .
   isn't / Japan / from / he

2. ___ ___ ___ ___ ___ ?
   ? / they / England / from / are

3. ___ ___ ___ ___ ___
   name / is / ? / what / your

4. ___ ___ ___ ___ .
   we / France / aren't / from

5. ___ ___ ___ ___ .
   I / am / Mexico / from

## Complete the sentences.

1. Akiko _____ from Japan.

2. Harry _____ from the USA.

3. Where _____ they from?

4. _____ is your name?

5. Michelle and Antoine _____ from England.

What • are • aren't • is • isn't

13

## How well did you do in this unit?
Write the CAN DO statement and assess yourself.
**Write 3, 2, or 1**
**3** = VERY WELL
**2** = WELL
**1** = NOT SO WELL

I CAN...
_____
_____
_____
_____
_____
_____
_____

Level THREE. Unit TWO.
*Let's play at home!*

2.1
Vocabulary

# Review the rooms in the house and family members

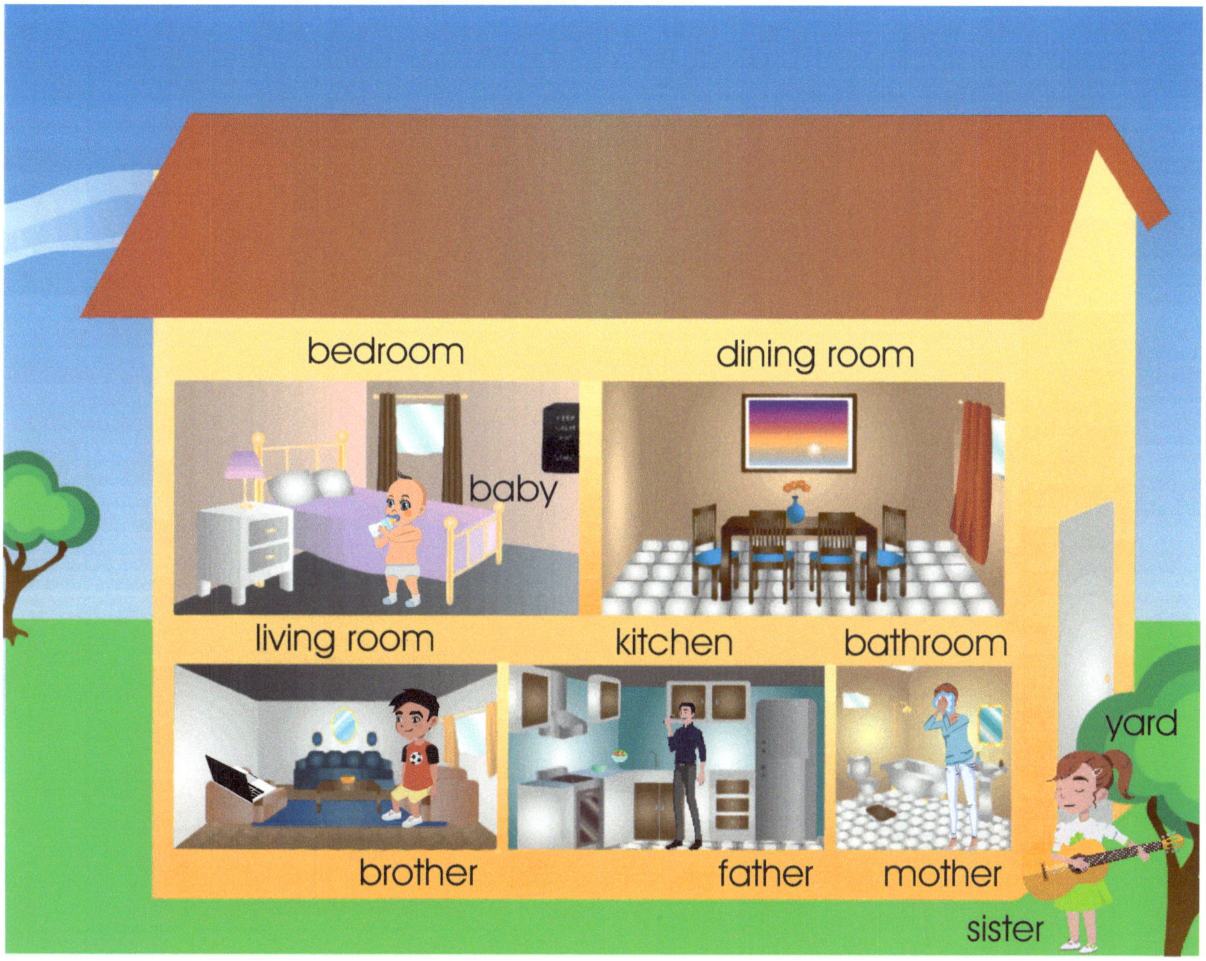

## 2.2 Dialogs

Level THREE. Unit TWO.
Let's play at home!

### Practice the dialogs

Where is mother?
-She is in the bathroom.
Is she washing her hands?
-No, she isn't. She's washing her face.

Where is father?
He's in the kitchen.
Is he eating a sandwich?
No, he isn't. He's eating salad.

Where is baby?
He's in the bedroom.
Is he sleeping?
No, he isn't. He's drinking milk.

Where is sister?
She's in the yard.
Is she playing soccer?
No, she isn't. She's playing the guitar.

Now you!

Where is _____?
He's in the _____.
Is he _____?
No, he isn't. He's _____.

**Level THREE. Unit TWO.**
Let's play at home!

2.3 Reading

## At home

All my family is at home today.
Father is in the kitchen, he's eating salad.
Mother is in the bathroom, she's washing her face.
Brother is in the living room, he's watching videos.
Sister is in the yard, she's playing the guitar.
Baby is in the bedroom, he's drinking milk.
And what am I doing? I am writing this story.
I love my family!

### Where are they?

1. Where is mother?
   ❑ kitchen ❑ yard ❑ bathroom
2. Where is father?
   ❑ kitchen ❑ yard ❑ bathroom
3. Where is sister?
   ❑ kitchen ❑ yard ❑ bathroom
4. Where is baby?
   ❑ bedroom ❑ yard
   ❑ living room
5. Where is brother?
   ❑ bedroom ❑ yard
   ❑ living room

### Answer the questions

1. What is mother doing?
   _____.
2. What is father doing?
   _____.
3. What is baby doing?
   _____.
4. What is sister doing?
   _____.
5. What is brother doing?
   _____.

**2.4 Writing**

Level THREE. Unit TWO.
*Let's play at home!*

Complete the text with the words from the box below. In any order you think necessary.

At home

All my family is at home today.
Father is in the _____, he's _____.
Mother is in the _____, she's _____.
Brother is in the _____, he's _____.
Sister is in the _____, she's _____.
Baby is in the _____, he's _____.
And what am I doing? I am _____.
I love my family!

kitchen • living room • yard • bedroom • bathroom
washing face • eating salad • drinking milk
watching videos • playing guitar • writing the story

### Level THREE. Unit TWO.
*Let's play at home!*

2.5 Language in use

**Present Progressive Tense.**
The present progressive tense expresses a current action, an action in progress.

We use the verb BE as a helping verb.
In sentences with HE, SHE, IT we use the verb IS.

To make a question we put IS before the pronoun.
Is he coloring?
To make negative sentences we use
IS + NOT
He is not (isn't) playing.

Change the sentences into questions

1. Mother is in the bathroom.
_____?
2. Father is in the kitchen.
_____?
3. Brother is in the living room.
_____?
4. Sister is in the yard.
_____?
5. Baby is the bedroom.
_____?

Change the sentences into negative

1. Mother is in the bathroom.
_____.
2. Father is in the kitchen.
_____.
3. Brother is in the living room.
_____.
4. Sister is in the yard.
_____.
5. Baby is the bedroom.
_____.

## How well did you do in this unit?
Write the CAN DO statement and assess yourself.
**Write 3, 2, or 1**
**3** = VERY WELL
**2** = WELL
**1** = NOT SO WELL

I CAN...
_____
_____
_____
_____
_____
_____
_____

**Level THREE Unit THREE**
*Let's play with animals!*

3.1 Vocabulary

## Review the animals and where they live

### FARM

 donkey

 horse

 cow

### ZOO

 tiger

 lion

 bear

### HOME

 cat

 dog

 hamster

## 3.2 Dialogs

**Level THREE Unit THREE**
*Let's play with animals!*

### Practice the dialogs

What is that?
-It's a lion.
Does a lion live in the farm?
-No, it doesn't. It lives in the zoo.

What are those?
-Those are donkeys.
Do donkeys live in the zoo?
-No, they don't. They live in the farm.

What is that?
-It's a cow.
Does a cow live in the zoo?
-No, it doesn't. It lives in the farm.

What are those?
-Those are cats.
Do cats live in the zoo?
-No, they don't. They live in a home.

What is that?
-It's a hamster.
Does a hamster live in the farm?
-No, it doesn't. It lives in a home.

*Now you!*

What are those?
-Those are _____.
Do _____ live in the _____?
-No, they don't. They live in a _____.

What is that?
-It's a _____.
Does a _____ live in the _____?
-No, it doesn't. It lives in a _____.

Level THREE Unit THREE
Let's play with animals!

## Animals, animals, animals!

Different animals live in different places.
Lions, tigers and bears don't live in homes and they don't live in farms. Where do they live?
They live in the zoo.
Horses, donkeys and cows don't live in homes, and they don't live in the zoo. Where do they live?
They live in the farm.
Cats, dogs and hamsters don't live in the zoo and they don't live in the farm. Where do they live?
They live in homes.
What animals live in your home?

### Answer the questions

1. The lion lives in the:
   ❏ zoo  ❏ farm  ❏ home
2. The hamster lives in the:
   ❏ zoo  ❏ farm  ❏ home
3. Cats live in the:
   ❏ zoo  ❏ farm  ❏ home
4. Bears live in the:
   ❏ zoo  ❏ farm  ❏ home
5. The donkey lives in the:
   ❏ zoo  ❏ farm  ❏ home

### Read the sentences
### Circle true (✓) or false (✗)

1. Bears live in the home.
   ✓   ✗
2. Cats live in the zoo.
   ✓   ✗
3. Lions live in the farm.
   ✓   ✗
4. The hamster lives in the home.
   ✓   ✗
5. The cow lives in the farm.
   ✓   ✗
6. The horse lives in the farm.
   ✓   ✗

**Level THREE Unit THREE**
*Let's play with animals!*

Complete the reading with the words from the box below

Animals, animals, animals!

Different animals live in different places.
Lions don't live in the _____
and they don't live in the _____.
Where do they live? They live in the _____.
Dogs don't live in the _____,
and they don't live in the _____.
Where do they live? They live in the _____.
A cow doesn't live in the _____
and it doesn't live in the _____.
Where does it live? It lives in the _____.

What is your favorite animal, where does it live?

farm (x3) • zoo (x3) • home (x3)

**Level THREE Unit THREE**
*Let's play with animals!*

3.5 Language in use

**Present Simple Tense**
We can express habits, customs and routines with the Present Simple Tense.

In the third person singular we add an „S"
at the end of the verb.
We use the helping verb DO / DOES to make interrogative sentences.
We use the helping verb DO / DOES + NOT to make negative sentences.

Choose the correct word

1. Lions _____ in the zoo.
   • live    • lives

2. _____ tigers live in the zoo?
   • Do    • Does

3. Where _____ a bear live?
   • do    • does

4. A hamster _____ live in the farm.
   • don't    • doesn't

5. Cats _____ live in the zoo.
   • don't    • doesn't

6. Where _____ cows live?
   • do    • doesn't

Write the words to complete the sentences

1. A lion _____ live in the farm.

2. Cats _____ live in the zoo.

3. _____ a horse live in the farm?

4. _____ donkeys live in the farm?

5. A dog _____ in the home.

6. Bears _____ in the zoo.

do • does • live
lives • doesn't • don't

# How well did you do in this unit?
Write the CAN DO statement and assess yourself.
**Write 3, 2, or 1**
**3** = VERY WELL
**2** = WELL
**1** = NOT SO WELL

I CAN...
_____
_____
_____
_____
_____
_____
_____

**Level THREE Unit FOUR**
*Let's CELEBRATE!*

Learn the year celebrations!

January     February     March     April

May     June     July     August

September     October     November     December

**4.2 Dialogs**

Level THREE Unit FOUR
*Let's CELEBRATE!*

Practice the dialogs

Mother's Day is going to be next week, are you ready?
-Sure!

-Halloween is going to be next Tuesday, are you ready?
-Almost!

Thanksgiving is going to be next month, are you ready?
-No, not yet!

The Christmas Ball is going to be next weekend, are you ready?
-Of course!

Valentine's Day is going to be next Friday, are you ready?
-Totally!

_____ is going to be next _____, are you ready?
- _____!

Now you!

**Level THREE Unit FOUR**
*Let's CELEBRATE!*

### Let's celebrate!

Next year I am going to have fun at many celebrations.
We are going to start on January 1st,
we are going to celebrate New Year's Day.
On February 14th, we are going to celebrate
Valentine's Day at school.
In May, I am going to dance in a Mother's Day festival.
Halloween is going to be fun, I am going to dress up
as a Super-Hero!
In November my family and I are going to visit my grandma
and we are going to eat a big Thanksgiving dinner.
And the last celebration is on December 25th,
Christmas Day, I love Christmas!
What celebration is your favorite?

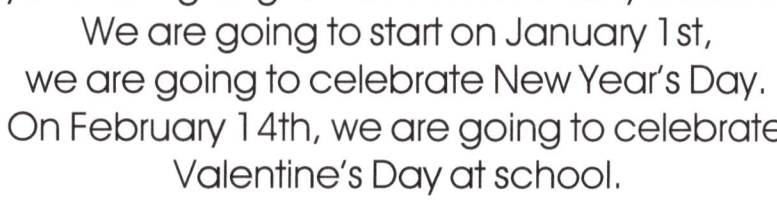

### What holiday is it?

1. December 25th is:
   - ☐ Christmas Day
   - ☐ Valentine's Day
   - ☐ Halloween

2. May 10th is:
   - ☐ Christmas Day
   - ☐ Mother's Day
   - ☐ Halloween

3. 3rd Thursday in November is:
   - ☐ Mother's Day
   - ☐ Valentine's Day
   - ☐ Thanksgiving

4. February 14th is:
   - ☐ Valentine's Day
   - ☐ Thanksgiving
   - ☐ Mother's Day

### Read the sentences.
Circle true ( ✔ ) or false ( ✘ )

1. Christmas is December 25th.
   ✔    ✘

2. New Year's Day is in November.
   ✔    ✘

3. Mother's Day is in May.
   ✔    ✘

4. Valentine's Day is in January.
   ✔    ✘

5. Halloween is October, 31st.
   ✔    ✘

## 4.4 Writing

**Level THREE Unit FOUR**
*Let's CELEBRATE!*

Complete the reading with the words from the box below. Choose the correct holiday.

Let's celebrate!

Next year I am going to have fun at many celebrations. We are going to start on January 1st, we are going to celebrate _____.
On February 14th, we are going to celebrate _____ at school.
In May, I am going to dance in a _____ festival.
_____ is going to be fun, I am going to dress up as a Super-Hero!
In November my family and I are going to visit my grandma and we are going to eat a big _____ dinner.
And the last celebration is on December 25th, _____. I love it!

What celebration is your favorite?

Christmas • Halloween • Mother´s Day • New Year´s Day
Valentine´s Day • Thanksgiving Day

**Level THREE Unit FOUR**
*Let's CELEBRATE!*

### 4.5 Language in use

**Future Tense**
**Affirmative**
BE + going to + verb

We use BE + going to + verb to express a planned action in the future.

Affirmative sentences:
I am going to dress-up as a super hero!
We are going to visit grandma.
She is going to dance in the festival.

## Time to Rhyme!

Hey diddle diddle,
The cat and the fiddle,
The cow jumped over the moon,
The little dog laughed
To see such fun,
And the dish ran away with the spoon!

### Unscramble the sentences

1. __ __ __ __ __
going to / next weekend / is Christmas / be

2. __ __ __ __ __
Next Friday / going to / Valentine's Day / be

3. __ __ __ __ __ __ .
is / Thanksgiving / going to / next month / be

4. __ __ __ __ __
next week / be / going to / is Mother's Day

# How well did you do in this unit?
Write the CAN DO statement and assess yourself.
**Write 3, 2, or 1**
**3** = VERY WELL
**2** = WELL
**1** = NOT SO WELL

I CAN...
_____
_____
_____
_____
_____
_____
_____

**Level THREE Unit FIVE**
*Let's play with food!*

**5.1** Vocabulary

## Learn the names of the food!

## Find the words

| X | D | P | E | P | W | C | S | D | Y |
|---|---|---|---|---|---|---|---|---|---|
| F | L | A | K | G | H | Q | A | E | J |
| I | C | Q | E | I | G | L | N | C | P |
| S | W | S | C | R | A | S | D | I | R |
| H | E | K | N | S | B | D | W | U | S |
| F | E | W | A | T | E | R | I | J | W |
| N | L | A | E | R | E | C | C | O | M |
| D | J | P | F | W | H | W | H | E | Q |
| F | N | I | V | Z | L | J | A | Y | N |
| I | F | A | M | Z | X | T | F | K | H |

BREAD
CEREAL
CHICKEN
EGGS
FISH
JUICE
MEAT
SALAD
SANDWICH
WATER

# 5.2 Dialogs

**Level THREE Unit FIVE**
*Let's play with food!*

## Practice the dialogs

Are you going to eat our delicious sandwich and water?
-Yes, I am. Thank you.

Are Lucy and Tony going to eat the delicious eggs and bread?
-Yes, they are. Thank you.

Are you and Andy going to choose our delicious chicken and salad?
-Yes, we are. Thank you.

Is Sandy going to have fish and water?
-Yes, she is. Thank you.

Is Harry going to taste our delicious meat and juice?
-Yes, he is. Thank you.

**Now you!**

Is/Are _____ going to _____ _____?
-Yes, ___ ___ . Thank you.

Level THREE Unit FIVE
*Let's play with food!*

**5.3 Reading**

## The delicious restaurant

My friends and I are going to celebrate my birthday at the "Delicious Restaurant". It is our favorite place to eat! Lucy and Tony are going to eat eggs and bread. Andy is going to choose chicken and salad. Sandy is going to have fish and water. Harry is going to taste meat and juice. Akiko and Tom are going to have cereal and juice. And I am going to have my favorite, a sandwich and tasty water! I love the Delicious Restaurant it is my favorite place to eat.

### What are they gong to eat?

1. Andy is going to choose:
   ❏ chicken and salad
   ❏ fish and water
   ❏ cereal and juice
2. Lucy and Tony are going to eat:
   ❏ fish and salad.
   ❏ eggs and bread
   ❏ cereal and juice
3. Harry is going to taste:
   ❏ cereal and juice
   ❏ fish and juice
   ❏ meat and juice
4. Akiko and Tom are going to have:
   ❏ cereal and juice
   ❏ chicken and salad
   ❏ eggs and bread

### Match the sentences with the food

1. Andy is going to choose: (___)
2. Lucy and Tony are going to eat: (___)
3. Harry is going to eat: (___)
4. Akiko and Tom are going to have: (___)
5. I am going to have: (___)

   a) Meat and juice
   b) Sandwich and water
   c) Eggs and bread
   d) Chicken and salad
   e) Cereal and juice

**5.4 Writing**

Level THREE Unit FIVE
*Let's play with food!*

Complete the reading with the words from the box below

The delicious restaurant

My friends and I are going to celebrate my birthday at the "Delicious Restaurant".
It is our favorite place to eat!
Lucy and Tony are going to eat _____.
Andy is going to choose _____.
Sandy is going to have _____. Harry is going to taste _____.
Akiko and Tom are going to have _____.
And I am going to have my favorite, a _____!
I love the Delicious Restaurant it is my favorite place to eat.

Chicken and salad • Eggs and bread • Meat and juice
Cereal and juice • Sandwich and water • Fish and water

**Level THREE Unit FIVE**
*Let's play with food!*

We use BE + going to + verb to express a planned action in the future.

We make interrogative sentences:
BE + subject + going to + verb?
Are you going to eat bread and juice?
Are they going to have fish and juice?
Is she going to choose cereal and juice?

Write a short affirmative answer

1. Are they going to eat fish?
   _____ _____ _____

2. Are you and Andy going to choose eggs?
   _____ _____ _____

3. Are you going to eat chicken?
   _____ _____ _____

4. Is Sandy going to have a sandwich?
   _____ _____ _____

5. Is Tony going to drink water?
   _____ _____ _____

Unscramble the sentences

1. ___ ___ ___ ___ ___ ___?
   a sandwich/eat/going/to/you/are

2. ___ ___ ___ ___ ___ ?
   they/eat/going to/eggs/are

3. ___ ___ ___ ___ ___ ?
   chicken/going to/you/are choose

4. ___ ___ ___ ___ ___ ?
   fish/going to/she /is/have

5. ___ ___ ___ ___ ___ ?
   they/are/going to/cereal have

## How well did you do in this unit?

Write the CAN DO statement and assess yourself.

**Write 3, 2, or 1**

**3** = VERY WELL

**2** = WELL

**1** = NOT SO WELL

I CAN...

_____

_____

_____

_____

_____

_____

**Level THREE Unit SIX**
*Let's play at school!*

6.1 Vocabulary

# Learn the names of the school supplies!

- book
- notebook
- pencil
- sharpener
- eraser
- crayons
- marker
- color pencils
- ruler
- pen

## 6.2 Dialogs

**Level THREE Unit SIX**
*Let's play at school!*

Practice the dialogs

Is Sandy going to write with a pen tomorrow?
-Yes, she is.
-She isn't going to write with a pencil.

Is Lucy going to color with color pencils tomorrow?
-Yes, she is.
-She isn't going to color with crayons.

Is Tony going to use a new sharpener tomorrow?
-Yes, he is.
-He isn't going to use a new eraser.

Are you going to work in the book tomorrow?
-Yes, I am.
-I'm not going to work in the notebook.

Are you going to _____ tomorrow?
-Yes, I am.
-I'm not going to _____.

**Level THREE Unit SIX**
*Let's play at school!*

**6.3 Reading**

## Busy day at school

Tomorrow is going to be a busy day at school.
Sandy isn't going to write with a pencil
but she is going to write with a pen.
Lucy isn't going to color with crayons
but she's going to color with color pencils.
Tony isn't going to use a new eraser
but he's going to use a new sharpener.
Andy isn't going to borrow a marker
but he's going to borrow a ruler.
And, I am not going to work in the notebook
but I am going to work in the book.
Yes, tomorrow is going to be a very busy day at school!

### What are they going to do tomorrow?

1. Is Sandy going to write with a pencil?
   ❏ Yes, she is.  ❏ No, she isn't.
2. Is Lucy going to color with color pencils?
   ❏ Yes, she is.  ❏ No, she isn't.
3. Is Tony going to use a new eraser?
   ❏ Yes, she is.  ❏ No, she isn't.
4. Is Andy going to borrow a marker?
   ❏ Yes, she is.  ❏ No, she isn't.
5. Are you going to work in the book?
   ❏ Yes, I am.  ❏ No, I'm not.

### Answer true or false

1. Sandy is going to write with a pencil.
   ❏ True  ❏ False
2. Lucy is going to color with color pencils.
   ❏ True  ❏ False
3. Tony is going to use a new sharpener.
   ❏ True  ❏ False
4. Andy is going to borrow a ruler.
   ❏ True  ❏ False
5. I am going to work in the book.
   ❏ True  ❏ False

**Level THREE Unit SIX**
*Let's play at school!*

Choose a word from the box below and fill in a blank. Then read aloud.

### Busy day at school

Tomorrow is going to be a busy day at school.
Sandy isn't going to write with a _____;
she is going to write with a _____.
Lucy isn't going to color with _____;
she's going to color with _____.
Tony isn't going to use a new _____;
he's going to use a new _____.
Andy isn't going to borrow a _____;
he's going to borrow a _____.
And, I am not going to work in the _____;
I am going to work in the _____.
Yes, tomorrow is going to be a very busy day at school!

---

pen • pencil • eraser • sharpener • book
notebook • markers • color penciis
crayons • ruler

## Level THREE Unit SIX
### Let's play at school!

6.5 Language in use

We use BE + going to + verb to express a planned action in the future.

We make negative sentences:
Subject + BE + NOT + going to + verb.
She is not going to use a pencil.
They are not going to use an eraser.
I am not going to work in the notebook.

### Answer the questions

1. Is Sandy going to write with a pen?
_____
2. Is Lucy going to color with crayons?
_____
3. Is Tony going to use a new eraser?
_____
4. Is Andy going to borrow a marker?
_____
5. Are you going to work in the notebook?
_____

### Choose the correct negative form

1. She _____ going to color with crayons.
   a) isn't     b) aren't
2. They _____ going to write with a pencil.
   a) isn't     b) aren't
3. He _____ to use a new eraser.
   a) am not   b) isn't
4. We _____ going to borrow a marker.
   a) am not   b) aren't
5. I _____ going to work in the book.
   a) aren't    b) am not

## How well did you do in this unit?
Write the CAN DO statement and assess yourself.
**Write 3, 2, or 1**
**3** = VERY WELL
**2** = WELL
**1** = NOT SO WELL

I CAN...
_____
_____
_____
_____
_____
_____
_____

**Level THREE Unit SEVEN**
*Let's play with countries!*

Learn the names of the countries

mountains

city

beach

**7.2 Dialogs**

Level THREE Unit SEVEN
Let's play with countries!

## Practice the dialogs

Where is Sandy going to go on her vacation?
-She is going to go to Puerto Rico.
Great! What is she going to do there?
-She's going to visit the beach.

Where are you going to go on your vacation?
-I am going to go to China.
Really? What are you going to do there?
-I'm going to visit the cities.

Where is Lucy going to go on her vacation?
-She is going to go to South Africa.
Awesome! What is she going to do there?
-She's going to visit the cities.

Where is Miss Patty going to go on her vacation?
-She's going to go to Australia.
Fantastic! What is she going to do there?
-She's going to visit the beach.

Where is Tony going to go on his vacation?
-He's going to go to Canada.
Great! What is he going to do there?
-He's to visit the mountains.

Where is _____ going to go on his/her vacation?
-He's/She's going to go to _____.
Fantastic! What is he/she going to do there?
-He/ She's going to visit _____.

46

**Level THREE Unit SEVEN**
Let's play with countries!

**7.3 Reading**

## Our next vacation

Miss Patty says that we are going to travel all around the world for our next vacation, well, with our imagination!
Andy is going to go to China; he's going to visit the cities.
Sandy is going to go to Puerto Rico; she's going to visit the beach.
Lucy is going to go to South Africa; she's going to visit the cities.
Tony is going to go to Canada; he's going to visit the mountains.
Miss Patty is going to go to Australia; she's going to visit the beach.
Yes, we are going to have awesome vacations, in our imagination!
Where are you going on your next vacation?

### Where are they going ?

1. Who is going to go to China?
   ☐ Andy   ☐ Lucy   ☐ Tony

2. Who is going to go to Canada?
   ☐ Miss Patty  ☐ Lucy   ☐ Tony

3. Who is going to go to Australia?
   ☐ Miss Patty  ☐ Tony   ☐ Andy

4. Who is going to go to Puerto Rico?
   ☐ Sandy   ☐ Lucy   ☐ Miss Patty

5. Who is going to go to South Africa?
   ☐ Andy   ☐ Tony   ☐ Lucy

### Match the sentence halves

1. Andy is going to visit        (____)
2. Sandy is going to visit       (____)
3. Lucy is going to visit        (____)
4. Tony is going to visit        (____)
5. Miss Patty is going to visit  (____)

a) the beach in Australia.
b) the beach in Puerto Rico.
c) the cities in China.
d) the cities in South Africa.
e) the mountains in Canada.

**Level THREE Unit SEVEN**
*Let's play with countries!*

Complete the reading with the words from the box below

**Our next vacation**

Miss Patty says that we are going to travel all around the world for our next vacation, well, with our imagination!
Andy is going to go to _____;
he's going to visit the _____.
Sandy is going to go to _____;
she's going to visit the _____.
Lucy is going to go to _____;
she's going to visit the _____.
Tony is going to go to _____;
he's going to visit the _____.
Miss Patty is going to go to _____;
she's going to visit the _____.
Yes, we are going to have awesome vacations, in our imagination!
Where are you going on your next vacation?

Canada • Puerto Rico • China • South Africa
mountains • cities • beach

**Level THREE Unit SEVEN**
*Let's play with countries!*

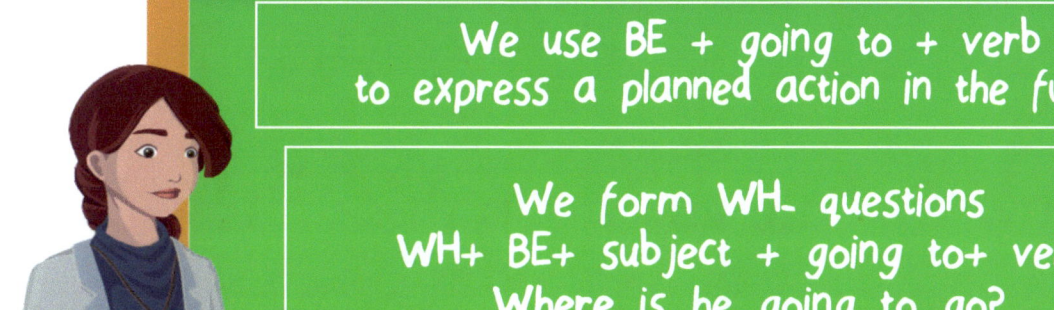

We use BE + going to + verb to express a planned action in the future.

We form WH- questions
WH+ BE+ subject + going to+ verb.
Where is he going to go?
What are they going to do?

## Unscramble the sentences

1. ____ ____ ____ ____ ____ ?
   Sandy / is / going to /where / go

2. ____ ____ ____ ____ ____ ?
   do / going to / Andy / is / what

3. ____ ____ ____ ____ ____ ?
   is / visit / who / China / going to

4. ____ ____ ____ ____ ____ ?
   Where / they / are / go / going to

## Complete the questions. Answer them using the clues in parenthesis

1. _____ is going to visit China? (Lucy)

2. _____ is Andy going to go?(China)

3. _____ are they going to do there? (visit the cities)

4. _____ is going to visit Canada? (Sandy)

5. _____ is Lucy going to go? (South Africa)

6. _____ are you going to do there? (go to the beach)

# How well did you do in this unit?
Write the CAN DO statement and assess yourself.
**Write 3, 2, or 1**
**3** = VERY WELL
**2** = WELL
**1** = NOT SO WELL

I CAN...
_____
_____
_____
_____
_____
_____

**Level THREE Unit EIGHT**
*Let's play after school!*

**8.1** Vocabulary

## Learn the school subjects

## Learn the after school activities

go to the movies

listen to music

play video games

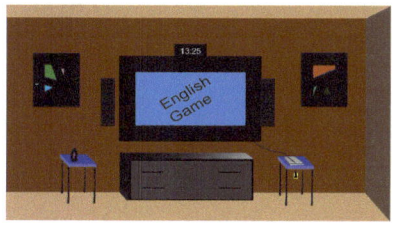

walk

watch T.V.

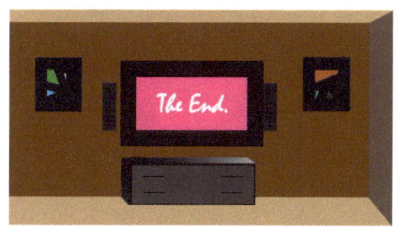

51

## 8.2 Dialogs

**Level THREE Unit EIGHT**
*Let's play after school!*

### Practice the dialogs

Can Tony go to the movies today?
-No, he can't. He has to study Math.

Can Lucy listen to music today?
-No, she can't. She has to study English.

Can Andy play video games today?
-No, he can't. He has to study Science.

Can Sandy watch TV today?
-No, she can't. She has to study Biology.

Can you go for a walk today?
-No, I can't. I have to prepare a history exam.

Now you!

Can _____ _____?
-No, she/he can't.
-She/he has to study _____.

**Level THREE Unit EIGHT**
Let's play after school!

**8.3 Reading**

## Exams

My friends and I are very busy today.
We can't do our usual activities.
We have to study because we have exams this week!
Tony can't go to the movies; he has to study Math.
Sandy can't watch TV today; she has to study Biology.
Andy can't play video games; he has to study Science.
Lucy can't listen to music; she has to study English.
Even Miss Patty can't go for a walk;
she has to prepare a History exam!
We all have to study very hard today!
What do you have to study?

### Choose true or false

1. Tony can't go to the movies. He has to study English.
   ❑ True   ❑ False
2. Sandy can't watch TV. She has to study Biology.
   ❑ True   ❑ False
3. Andy can't play video games. He has to study History.
   ❑ True   ❑ False
4. Lucy can't listen to music. She has to study Science.
   ❑ True   ❑ False
5. Miss Patty can't go for a walk. She has to study History.
   ❑ True   ❑ False

### Choose the correct activity

1. Sandy has to study:
   ❑ Math  ❑ Biology  ❑ History
2. Andy has to study:
   ❑ Math  ❑ Biology  ❑ Science
3. Lucy has to study:
   ❑ English  ❑ Math  ❑ History
4. Tony has to study:
   ❑ English  ❑ Math  ❑ History
5. Miss Patty has to study:
   ❑ English  ❑ Science  ❑ History

**8.4 Writing**

Level THREE Unit EIGHT
Let's play after school!

Complete the reading with the words from the box below

Exams

My friends and I are very busy today.
We can't do our usual activities.
We have to study because we have exams this week!
Tony can't _____; he has to study _____.
Sandy can't _____ today; she has to study _____.
Andy can't _____; he has to study _____.
Lucy can't _____; she has to study _____.
Even Miss Patty can't _____;
she has to prepare a _____ exam!
We all have to study very hard today!
What do you have to study?

go to the movies • listen to music • play video games
watch TV • walk

Math • History • Biology • English • Science

**Level THREE Unit EIGHT**
Let's play after school!

**8.5 Language in use**

We use have to and has to, to express an obligation or a necessity.
We use CAN in the Present Simple tense to express ability.

We form sentences with have to and has to in the Present Simple tense affirmative form: Subject + have/has to + verb
We use have to with: I, you, we they
We use has to with: he, she, it.

We use CAN with every subject:
I/you/he/she/it/we/they CAN.
To make interrogative sentences:
CAN + subject + verb (simple form)
To make negative sentences:
Subject + CAN + NOT + can't + verb (simple form)

## Time to Rhyme!

Now I lay me down to sleep
I pray the Lord my soul to keep;
If I should die before I wake,
I pray the Lord my soul to take.
Your love be with me through the night,
And wake me with the morning light.

## Answer the questions

1. Can Tony go to the movies?
   No, ____ ____.
   He ____ ____ study Math.

2. Can Andy play video games today?
   No, ____ ____.
   He ____ ____ study Science.

3. Can Lucy listen to music?
   No, ____ ____.
   She ____ ____ study English.

4. Can you go for a walk today?
   No, ____ ____. I ____ ____ prepare a History exam.

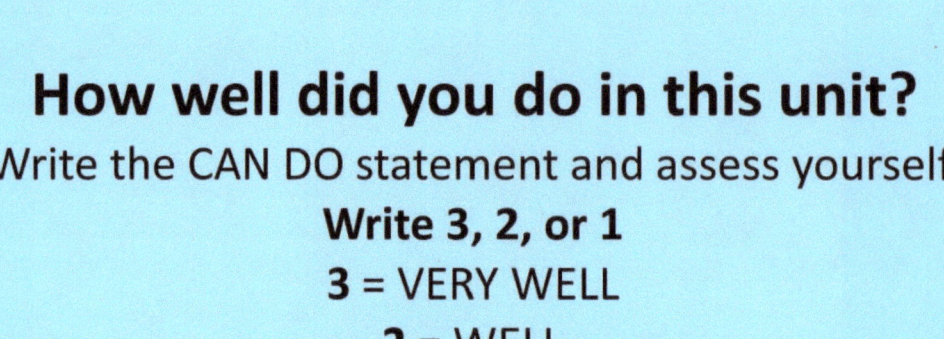

**How well did you do in this unit?**
Write the CAN DO statement and assess yourself.
**Write 3, 2, or 1**
**3** = VERY WELL
**2** = WELL
**1** = NOT SO WELL

I CAN...
_____
_____
_____
_____
_____
_____
_____

**Level THREE Unit NINE**
*Let's play with the weather!*

9.1 Vocabulary

## Learn the clothes and the weather

**rainy** — raincoat

**snowy** — boots

**sunny** — shorts

**cloudy** — sweater

**windy** — jacket

57

**9.2 Dialogs**

Level THREE Unit NINE
*Let's play with the weather!*

## Practice the dialogs

Do I have to wear a raincoat?
-Yes, you do. It's rainy.

Do Andy and Tony have to wear sweaters?
-Yes, they do. It's cloudy.

Does Tony have to wear boots?
-Yes, he does. It's snowy.

Does Lucy have to wear shorts?
-Yes, she does. It's sunny.

Do you and Sandy have to wear jackets?
-Yes, we do. It's windy.

Do/Does _____ have to wear _____?
-Yes, _____ _____. It's _____.

**Level THREE Unit NINE**
*Let's play with the weather!*

**9.3 Reading**

### Different clothes for different weather

Our teacher, Miss Patty, says that we have to wear different clothes for different kinds of weather.
She says that, we have to wear a jacket when it's windy. We have to wear a raincoat when it's rainy. We have to wear a sweater when it's cloudy. We have to wear boots when it's snowy. And we have to wear shorts when it's sunny. Well, it is sure a lot to remember, but we are happy because we have Miss Patty to tell us what clothes to wear in different kinds of weather.
What do you have to wear today?

Circle ( ✓ ) for true
Circle ( ✗ ) for false

Choose the correct clothes

1. It's rainy.
   I have to wear shorts.
   ✓   ✗

2. It's cloudy.
   They have to wear a sweater.
   ✓   ✗

3. It's snowy.
   He has to wear sweater.
   ✓   ✗

4. It's sunny.
   She has to wear a raincoat.
   ✓   ✗

5. It's windy.
   We have to wear jackets.
   ✓   ✗

1. It's rainy. I have to wear ____.
   • sweater   • raincoat   • jacket

2. It's cloudy. They have to wear ____.
   • sweater   • raincoat   • shorts

3. It's snowy. He has to wear ____.
   • shorts   • raincoat   • boots

4. It's sunny. She has to wear ____.
   • shorts   • raincoat   • boots

5. It's windy. We have to wear ____.
   • boots   • jackets   • shorts

## 9.4 Writing

**Level THREE Unit NINE**
*Let's play with the weather!*

Complete the reading with the words from the box below

### Different clothes for different weather

Our teacher, Miss Patty, says that we have to wear different clothes for different kinds of weather.
She says that, we have to wear a _____ when it's _____. We have to wear a _____ when it's _____. We have to wear a _____ when it's _____. We have to wear _____ when it's _____.
And we have to wear _____ when it's _____. Well, it is sure a lot to remember, but we are happy because we have Miss Patty to tell us what clothes to wear in different kinds of weather.
What do you have to wear today?
It's _____ I have to wear _____!

---

shorts • sweater • boots • jackets • raincoat (x2)
sunny • cloudy • snowy • windy • rainy (x2)

---

**Level THREE Unit NINE**
*Let's play with the weather!*

9.5 Language in use

We use have to and has to, to express an obligation or a necessity.

We form questions with have to and has to in the Present Simple tense:
Do / does + Subject + have to + verb

We use do / have to with: I, you, we, they
Do you have to wear a raincoat?

We use does / have to with: he, she, it
Does she have to wear boots?

**Complete the questions using the correct form of have to**

1. _____ I _____ _____ wear a raincoat?

2. _____ Andy and Tony _____ _____ wear sweaters?

3. _____ Tony _____ _____ wear boots?

4. _____ Lucy _____ _____ wear shorts?

5. _____ you _____ _____ wear a sweater?

**Complete clothes crosswords**

across

1     2     3

4     5     6

down

7     8

9     10

## How well did you do in this unit?
Write the CAN DO statement and assess yourself.
**Write 3, 2, or 1**
**3** = VERY WELL
**2** = WELL
**1** = NOT SO WELL

I CAN...
_____
_____
_____
_____
_____
_____
_____

**Level THREE Unit TEN**
*Let's play with seasons!*

## Learn the names of the clothes and the seasons of the year

**Level THREE Unit TEN**
Let's play with seasons!

## Practice the dialogs

I think I have to wear a scarf in the spring!
-Don't be silly!
You don't have to wear a scarf.
It's warm in the spring.

I think I have to wear gloves in the summer!
-Don't be silly!
You don't have to wear gloves.
It's hot in the summer.

I think I have to wear a swimsuit in the winter.
Don't be silly!
You don't have to wear a swimsuit.
It's cold in the winter.

I think I have to wear a T-shirt in the fall.
-Don't be silly!
You don't have to wear a T-shirt.
It's cool in the fall.

**Now you!**

I think I have to wear a _____ in the _____.
Don't be silly!
You don't have to wear a _____.
It's _____ in the _____.

**Level THREE Unit TEN**
*Let's play with seasons!*

## Silly clothes for different seasons

Today we are playing "dress up"
but we are being silly with clothes
that we have to wear in the different seasons.
Sandy chooses to wear gloves in the summer!
Miss Patty says: "Of course you can wear them,
but you don't have to wear gloves
because in the summer it is hot."
Andy chooses to wear a scarf in the spring!
"You don't have to wear a scarf because
in the spring it is warm."
Tony chooses to wear a swimsuit in the winter!
"You don't have to wear a swimsuit because
it is cold in the winter."
Lucy chooses to wear a T-shirt in the fall!
You don't have to wear a T-shirt because it is cool in the fall."
You don't have to wear silly clothes, but if you want to…
have fun!

Match sentences 1-4 with a-d

1) It's hot in the _____.
2) It's cold in the _____.
3) It's cool in the _____.
4) It's warm in the _____.

a)   b)   c)   d)

Circle true or false

1. You don't have to wear gloves in the winter        true        false
2. You don't have to wear a swimsuit in the summer    true        false
3. You don't have to wear a scarf in the spring       true        false
4. You don't have wear a T-shirt in the fall          true        false

# 10.4 Writing

Level THREE Unit TEN
*Let's play with seasons!*

Complete the reading with the words from the box below

### Silly clothes for different seasons

Today we are playing "dress up" but we are being silly with clothes that we have to wear in the different seasons.

Sandy chooses to wear _____ in the _____! Miss Patty says: "Of course you can wear that, but you don't have to."

Andy chooses to wear a _____ in the _____! "Of course you can wear that, but you don't have to."

Tony chooses to wear a _____ in the _____! "Of course you can wear that, but you don't have to."

Lucy chooses to wear a _____ in the _____! "Of course you can wear that, but you don't have to."

You don't have to wear silly clothes, but if you want to… have fun!

winter • spring • summer • fall
gloves • t-shirt • swimsuit • scarf

**Level THREE Unit TEN**
*Let's play with seasons!*

**10.5** Language in use

We use have to and has to, to express an obligation or a necessity.
When you use the negative form it express something that it is not necessary, but if you want you can do it.
You don't have to wear gloves in the summer (but if you want to, do it!)

We use do not / have to with: I, you, we, they
You don't have to wear gloves in the summer.
We use does not / have to with: he, she, it
She doesn't have to wear a swimsuit in the winter.

**Complete the words for clothes and seasons**

1. f ___ ___ ___
2. g ___ ___ ___ ___ s
3. s ___ ___ ___ f
4. s ___ ___ ___ ___ g
5. s ___ ___ ___ ___ r
6. s ___ ___ m ___ ___ ___ t
7. T - ___ ___ ___ ___ t
8. w ___ ___ ___ ___ r

**Unscramble the sentences**

1. _____ _____ _____ _____ _____ .
a scarf / have to / you / don't / wear

2. _____ _____ _____ _____ _____ .
a swimsuit / she / have to / doesn't / wear

3. _____ _____ _____ _____ _____ .
a T-shirt / don't / have to / wear / they

4. _____ _____ _____ _____ _____ .
doesn't / wear / have to / gloves / he

# How well did you do in this unit?
Write the CAN DO statement and assess yourself.
**Write 3, 2, or 1**
**3** = VERY WELL
**2** = WELL
**1** = NOT SO WELL

I CAN...
_____
_____
_____
_____
_____
_____
_____

**Level THREE Unit ELEVEN**
*Let's play with magic words!*

# Learn days of the week and months of the year

| 1 | 2 | 3 | 4 | 5 | 6 | 7 |
|---|---|---|---|---|---|---|
| Sunday | Monday | Tuesday | Wednesday | Thursday | Friday | Saturday |

| 1 | 2 | 3 | 4 | 5 | 6 |
|---|---|---|---|---|---|
| January | February | March | April | May | June |

| 7 | 8 | 9 | 10 | 11 | 12 |
|---|---|---|----|----|----|
| July | August | September | October | November | December |

THANK YOU

MAY I?

EXCUSE ME

You're welcome

I'M SORRY

PLEASE

May I borrow...?

Don't worry

Let me help you

69

## 11.2 Dialogs

**Level THREE Unit ELEVEN**
Let's play with magic words!

### Practice the dialogs

Excuse me, how do you spell OCTOBER?
-With a capital "O-c-t-o-b-e-r."
Thank you.
-You're welcome.

Excuse me, may I borrow your pencil?
-Sure!
Thanks.
-Don't worry.

I'm sorry, how do you spell MONDAY?
-With a capital "M-o-n-d-a-y."
Thanks.
-Don't worry.

May I borrow your marker, please?
-Of course!
Thank you.
-You're welcome.

Excuse me, how do you spell DECEMBER?
-With a capital "D-e-c-e-m-b-e-r."
Thank you.
-Sure.

Excuse me; may I borrow your book?
-Sure!
Thanks.
-You're welcome.

Excuse me, how do you spell _____?
-With a capital "__ __ __ __ __ __ __ __ __ __"
Thanks.
-You're welcome.

Excuse me; may I borrow your _____?
-Sure!
Thanks.
-You're welcome.

**Level THREE Unit ELEVEN**
Let's play with magic words!

## Magic words

**THANK YOU**  **EXCUSE ME**

Miss Patty says that there are some beautiful words that we have to use every day. She calls them "Magic Words"; she says that when we use them everything is better, like MAGIC! For example, if you don't have a pencil, you don't just grab it. You can say: May I borrow your pencil? And then your friend is not going to be angry, he is going to let you use his pencil! Isn't it like magic? When you want to come into the classroom, if you say: May I come in? Miss Patty is going to be very happy; she is going to answer: "Sure!" You see, just like magic! There are other Magic Words like: please, excuse me, I'm sorry, don't worry; and Miss Patty's favorite: Let me help you! She is always so nice! Well, remember to always use Magic Words and everything is going to be MAGICAL!

*Let me help you*   **MAY I?**

**I'M SORRY**   **PLEASE**

*You're welcome*   *Don't worry*   *May I borrow...?*

Choose the best magic word to complete the expressions

1. May I borrow your pencil?
   ❑ You're welcome   ❑ May I come in?   ❑ Of course!

2. May I come in?
   ❑ Sure!   ❑ You're welcome   ❑ Thank you!

3. Let me help you!
   ❑ Thank you.   ❑ I'm sorry   ❑ May I come in?

4. _____, may I borrow your pencil?
   ❑ Thanks   ❑ You're welcome   ❑ Excuse me

## 11.4 Writing

**Level THREE Unit ELEVEN**
Let's play with magic words!

Choose a word from the box below and fill in a blank. Then read aloud.

### Magic words

In class every day we use special words,
they are called "Magic Words."
For example: _____, _____,
and _____.
We also use _____
Miss Patty says: _____
There are other Magic Words like:
_____, _____, _____ and _____.
My favorite word is: _____.
I am going to use Magic Words every day in school and at home.

What is your favorite Magic Word?

---

Excuse me • Thank you • You're welcome • Please
I'm sorry • May I come in? • Let me help you
May I borrow? • Don't worry • Sure

---

THANK YOU    EXCUSE ME    May I?

Let me help you    I'M SORRY    PLEASE

You're welcome    Don't worry

**Level THREE Unit ELEVEN**
*Let's play with magic words!*

11.5 Language in use

We use capital letters at the beginning of:
Days of the week
Sunday, Monday, Tuesday
Tomorrow is going to be Monday.
Months of the year:
January, February, March

## Complete the days of the week

1. ___ unday
2. ___ onday
3. T _____
4. W _____
5. ___ hursday,
6. F _____
7. _____ .

## Complete the months of the year

1. ___ anuary
2. ___ ebruary
3. M _____
4. ___ pril
5. _____
6. J _____
7. ___ uly
8. A _____
9. ___ eptember
10. Oct _____
11. N _____
12. _____

73

## How well did you do in this unit?
Write the CAN DO statement and assess yourself.
**Write 3, 2, or 1**
**3** = VERY WELL
**2** = WELL
**1** = NOT SO WELL

I CAN...
_____
_____
_____
_____
_____
_____
_____

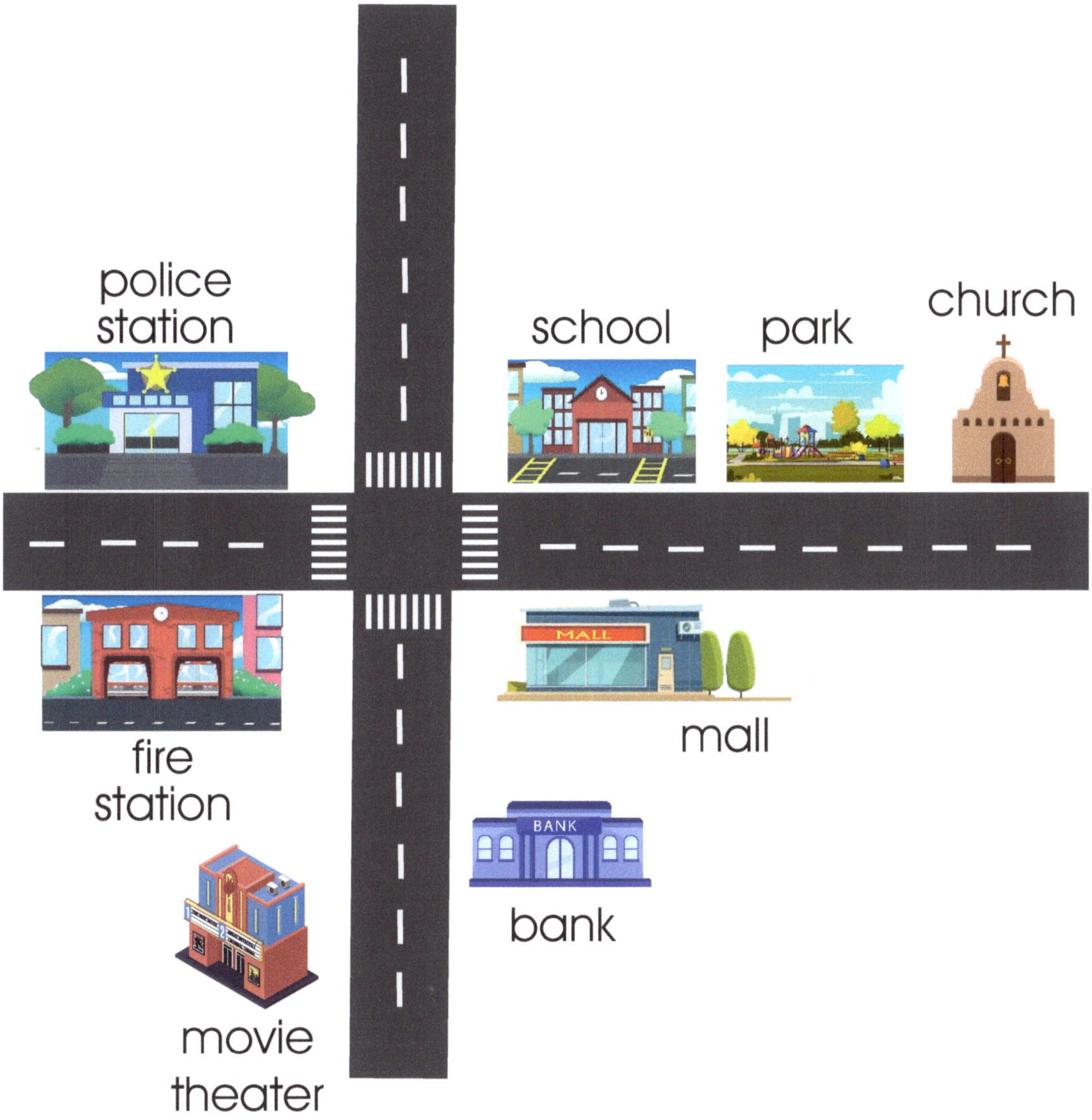

**Level THREE Unit TWELVE**
*Let's play around the city!*

**12.1**
Vocabulary

police station

school

park

church

fire station

mall

bank

movie theater

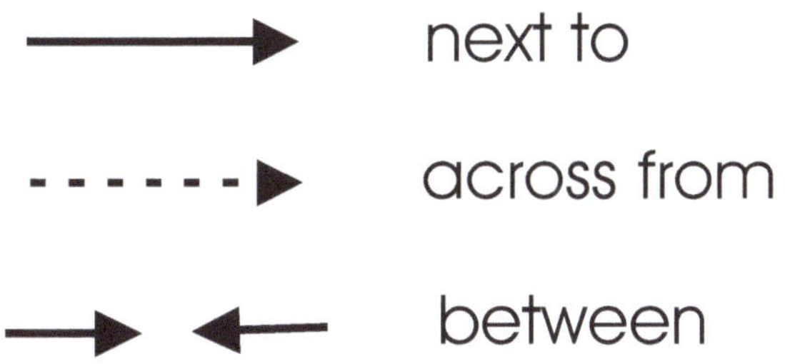

→ next to

┄┄► across from

→ ← between

## 12.2 Dialogs

**Level THREE Unit TWELVE**
*Let's play around the city!*

### Practice the dialogs

Excuse me, where is the mall?
-It's across from the park.
Thank you.
-Sure!

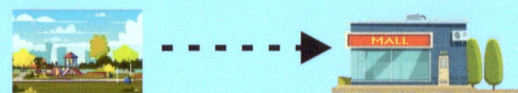

Excuse me, where is the school?
-It's next to the park.
Thanks.
-Sure.

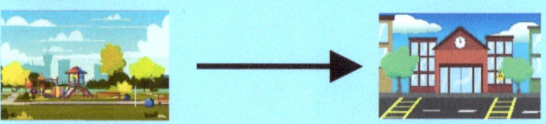

Excuse me, where is the fire station?
-It's across from the police station.
Thank you.
-Don't worry.

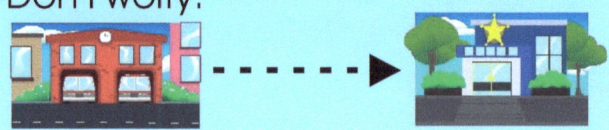

Excuse me, where is the bank?
-It's across from the movie theater.
Thank you.
-You're welcome.

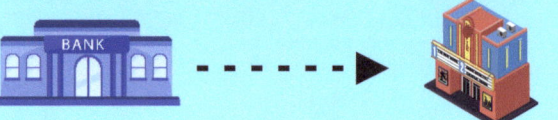

Sorry, where is the park?
-It's between the church and the school.
Thanks a lot.
-You're welcome.

Excuse me, where is the _____?
-It's _____.
Thank you.
-You're welcome

76

**Level THREE Unit TWELVE**
*Let's play around the city!*

## My town

I live in a beautiful town. My mom and dad take me everywhere. And now, I can tell my friends where everything is. For example; the mall, my favorite place in town, is across from the park; I love to go to the mall and then to the park on Saturdays. The park is between the church and the school. I can see the park from the window in my classroom. The police station is just across from the fire station. The bank is across from the movie theater. I love my town. My town is beautiful! Is your town beautiful? Do you know where everything is?

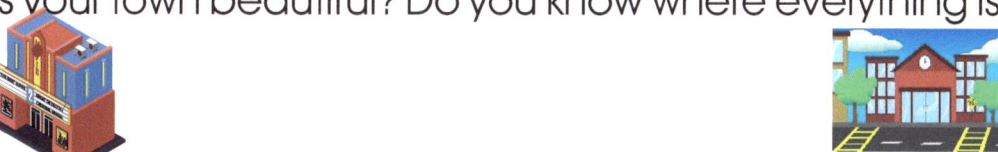

**Choose True** if the sentences are correct. **False** if the sentences are incorrect.

1. The mall is across from the fire station.
   ❏ True  ❏ False
2. The park is across from the mall.
   ❏ True  ❏ False
3. The church is between the school and the park.
   ❏ True  ❏ False
4. The movie theater is next to the bank.
   ❏ True  ❏ False

Match sentences 1-5 with images a-e

- The mall is across from the _____.
- The park is between the school and the _____.
- The park is next to the _____.
- The movie theater is across from the _____.
- The fire station is across from the _____.

**12.4 Writing**

Level THREE Unit TWELVE
Let's play around the city!

Choose a word from the box below and fill in a blank. Then read aloud.

### My town

I live in a beautiful town. My mom and dad take me everywhere.
And now, I can tell my friends where everything is.
For example: the _____, my favorite place in town,
is across from the _____.
The _____ is between the _____ and the _____.
The _____ is just across from the _____.
The _____ is across from the _____.
I love my town. My town is beautiful!
Is your town beautiful? Do you know where everything is?

fire station • police station • church • school
mall • park • bank • movie theater

**Level THREE Unit TWELVE**
*Let's play around the city!*

We use the imperative form to give directions.

We use the prepositions;
next to, across from and between
to express the relation of places to give directions.

On the corner turn right.
The school is across from the mall.
Turn left on the corner.
The mall is next to the park.
Turn right on the corner.
The movie theater is between the school and the park.

Unscramble the sentences

1. ____ ____ ____ ____.
next to / is / the school the park

2. ____ ____ ____ ____ ____.
right / the / on / corner turn

3. ____ ____ ____ ____ ____.
The park / between / is the church / and mall

4. ____ ____ ____ ____ ____.
corner / the / on / left / turn

5. ____ ____ ____ ____.
the mall / across from / is the bank

## Time to Rhyme

Wee Willie Winkie
Runs through the town,
Upstairs and downstairs,
In his nightgown,
Tapping at the window,
Crying through the lock,
Are all the children in their beds?
It's past eight o'clock!

## How well did you do in this unit?
Write the CAN DO statement and assess yourself.
**Write 3, 2, or 1**
**3** = VERY WELL
**2** = WELL
**1** = NOT SO WELL

I CAN...
_____
_____
_____
_____
_____
_____
_____

**Level THREE Unit THIRTEEN**
*Let's play with toys!*

13.1 Vocabulary

## Learn the names of the toys

- toy car
- truck
- blocks
- train
- teddy bear
- doll
- bike
- ball
- jump rope

### 13.2 Dialogs

Level THREE Unit THIRTEEN
Let's play with toys!

## Practice the dialogs

Is Andy going to play with his train?
-No, he isn't.
-He's going to play with his blocks.

Are you going to play with your Teddy Bear?
-No, I'm not. I'm going to ride my bike.

Is Sandy going to play with her ball?
-No, she isn't.
-She's going to play with her Teddy Bear.

Are Lucy and Sandy going to play with their dolls?
-No, they aren't. They're going to play with their jump ropes.

Are you and Tony going to play with your toy cars?
-No, we aren't.
-We are going to play with our trucks.

**Now you!**

Is / Are _____ going to play with _____ _____ ?
-No, _____ _____. _____ going to play with _____ _____.

**Level THREE Unit THIRTEEN**
*Let's play with toys!*

## What are you going to play with?

Tomorrow is going to be Saturday, and all my friends and I want to play all day long. But, what are we going to play with? Andy isn't going to play with his train; he's going to play with his blocks. Lucy isn't going to play with her dolls; she's going to play with her jump rope. Tony isn't going to play with his toy cars; he's going to play with his trucks. Sandy isn't going to play with her ball; she's going to play with her Teddy bear. And I'm not going to play with my jump rope; I'm going to play with my ball. Yes, my friends and I are going to have fun tomorrow!

What are you going to play with?

### What are you going to play with?

1. What is Andy going to play with?
   ❑ blocks  ❑ train  ❑ ball

2. What is Sandy going to play with?
   ❑ ball  ❑ teddy bear  ❑ jump rope

3. What is Lucy going to play with?
   ❑ dolls  ❑ trucks  ❑ jump rope

4. What is Tony going to play with?
   ❑ trucks  ❑ bike  ❑ toy cars

5. What are you going to play with?
   ❑ jump rope  ❑ ball  ❑ train

### Circle (✓) if the sentence is correct (✗) if it's incorrect

1. Sandy isn't going to play with her Teddy bear.
   ✓ True    ✗ False
2. Tony is going to play with his trucks.
   ✓ True    ✗ False
3. I am not going to play with jump rope.
   ✓ True    ✗ False
4. Andy is going to play with his train.
   ✓ True    ✗ False
5. Lucy isn't going to play with her jump rope.
   ✓ True    ✗ False

### 13.4 Writing

**Level THREE Unit THIRTEEN**
*Let's play with toys!*

Complete the reading with the words from the box below. Then read aloud.

What are you going to play with?
Tomorrow is going to be Saturday,
and all my friends and I want to play all day long.
But, what are we going to play with?
Andy isn't going to play with his _____;
he's going to play with his _____.
Lucy isn't going to play with her _____;
she's going to play with her _____.
Tony isn't going to play with his _____;
he's going to play with _____.
Sandy isn't going to play with her _____;
she's going to play with her _____.
And you, what are YOU going to play with?
I'm not going to play with my _____;
I'm going to play with my _____.

Yes, my friends and I are going to have fun tomorrow!

toys • bike • jump rope • toy car
doll • teddy bear • blocks • truck • train • ball

**Level THREE Unit THIRTEEN**
*Let's play with toys!*

We use BE + going to + verb to express a planned action in the future.

We use the Possessive Adjectives to indicate ownership.
*Note that the possessive adjective does not change if you own one or several things.
My train
My trains

I = my
you = your
he = his
she = her
it = its
we = our
they = their

**Complete the sentences with the correct possessive adjective**

1. Andy is going to play with _____ train.
2. Sandy isn't going to play with _____ dolls.
3. Tony and Andy aren't going to play with _____ toy cars.
4. Lucy and I are going to play with _____ jump ropes.
5. I'm not going to play with _____ ball.
6. You are going to play with _____ Teddy bear.

my • your • his • her • our • their

**Give a short answer**

1. Is Andy going to play with the train?
   -No, _____ _____.
2. Is Sandy going to play with the dolls?
   -Yes, _____ _____.
3. Are Tony and Andy going to play with the toy cars?
   -No, _____ _____.
4. Are you and Lucy going to play with the jump ropes?
   -Yes, _____ _____.
5. Are you going to play with the ball?
   -No, _____ _____.

# How well did you do in this unit?
Write the CAN DO statement and assess yourself.
**Write 3, 2, or 1**
**3** = VERY WELL
**2** = WELL
**1** = NOT SO WELL

I CAN...
_____
_____
_____
_____
_____
_____
_____

**Level THREE Unit FOURTEEN**
*Let's play with food!*

## Learn the names of the food

milk

soup

hot dogs

spaghetti

hamburger

pizza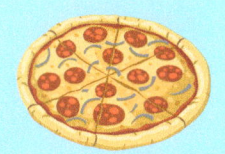

fries

bread

cookies

eggs

## Complete the food words

1. m___ ___ k
2. b___ ___ ___ d
3. c___ ___ k___ ___ ___
4. e___ ___ s
5. s___ ___ p
6. h___ ___ b___ ___ g___ ___
7. f___ ___ ___ s
8. h___ ___ d___ ___ s
9. p___ ___ ___ a
10. s___ ___ ___ h___ ___ ___ i

**14.2** Dialogs

Level THREE Unit FOURTEEN
Let's play with food!

## Practice the dialogs

What are you going to eat?
-I'm going to eat cookies.
Do you want milk too?
-Yes, thanks.

What are you going to eat?
-I'm going to eat spaghetti.
Do you want pizza too?
-Yes, please.

What are you going to eat?
-I'm going to eat eggs.
Do you want bread too?
-Sure, thanks.

What are you going to eat?
-I'm going to eat hot dogs.
Do you want soup too?
-No, thanks.

What are you going to eat?
-I'm going to eat hamburger.
Do you want fries too?
-No, thanks.

What are you going to eat?
-I'm going to eat _____.
Do you want _____ too?
-No, thanks. / Yes, please.

Level THREE Unit FOURTEEN
*Let's play with food!*

14.3 Reading

## Delicious Food

My friends and I are always hungry
when we get home from school.
Right now we are thinking
what we are going to eat this afternoon.
Sandy is going to eat cookies and milk.
Andy is going to eat spaghetti and pizza.
Lucy is going to eat eggs and bread.
Harry is going to eat a hamburger.
Tony is going to eat hot dogs.
We love to get home and eat delicious food.
Thank you mom! Thank you dad!
What are you going to eat?

Who is going to eat?
Sandy/Andy/Lucy/Tony/Harry

Circle True if the sentence is correct.
False if the sentence is incorrect.

1. Who is going to eat a hamburger?
   _____

2. Who is going to eat spaghetti and pizza?
   _____

3. Who is going to eat cookies and milk?
   _____

4. Who is going to eat eggs and bread?
   _____

5. Who is going to eat hot dogs?
   _____

1. Andy is going to eat spaghetti and pizza.
   True    False
2. Sandy is going to eat eggs and bread.
   True    False
3. Lucy is going to eat cookies and milk.
   True    False
4. Harry is going to eat a hamburger.
   True    False
5. Tony is going to eat soup.
   True    False

# 14.4 Writing

Complete the reading with the words from the box below

### Delicious Food

My friends and I are always hungry
when we get home from school.
Right now we are thinking what we are going to eat
this afternoon. Sandy is going to eat _____ and _____.
Andy is going to eat _____ and _____.
Lucy is going to eat _____ and _____.
Harry is going to eat a _____ and _____.
Tony is going to eat _____ and _____.
We love to get home and eat delicious food.
Thank you mom! Thank you dad!
What are you going to eat?
I am going to eat _____ and _____.,

eggs • bread • cookies • milk • spaghetti • pizza
hot dogs • hamburger • soup • fries

**Level THREE Unit FOURTEEN**
*Let's play with food!*

**14.5** Language in use

We use BE + going to + verb to express a planned action in the future.

We use WH - questions to ask for specific information.
Who = a person
What = a thing or action
When = a time
Where = a place

We form WH question in the future tense:
Wh + be + subject + going to + verb + complement?

**Complete the sentences with the WH question word Who/ What/ Where/ When**

1. _____ is Andy going to eat? (pizza)

2. _____ is going to eat pizza? (Sandy)

3. _____ are you going to eat cookies? (tomorrow)

4. _____ are they going to eat hamburgers? (in the kitchen)

**Unscramble the sentences**

1. ___ ___ ___ ___ ___ ?
What/ Andy/ going to/ is/ eat

2. ___ ___ ___ ___ ___ ?
going to/ is / who/ pizza/eat

3. ___ ___ ___ ___ ___ ___ ?
cookies/eat/ going to/ are when/you

4. ___ ___ ___ ___ ___ ___ ?
they/going to/ hamburgers eat/when/are

91

## How well did you do in this unit?
Write the CAN DO statement and assess yourself.
**Write 3, 2, or 1**
**3** = VERY WELL
**2** = WELL
**1** = NOT SO WELL

I CAN...
_____
_____
_____
_____
_____
_____
_____

**Level THREE Unit FIFTEEN**
*Let's play games and sports!*

## Learn the names of games and sports

soccer      football      basketball

baseball      volley ball      swimming

chess      checkers

jumping rope      tag

**Level THREE Unit FIFTEEN**
Let's play games and sports!

## Practice the dialogs

Are you going to play chess?
-No, I'm not.
What are you going to play?
-I think I'm going to play checkers.
Great! Can I play too?

Are you and Michelle going to jump rope?
-No, we aren't.
What are you going to play?
-Perhaps we're going to play tag.
Great! Can I play too?

Are Tony and Harry going to play soccer?
-No, they aren't.
What are they going to play?
-I guess they're going to play football.
Great! Can I play too?

Is Sandy going to play volleyball?
-No, she isn't.
What is she going to play?
-I think she's going to go swimming.
Great! Can I go too?

Is Sandy going to play _____?
-No, she isn't.
What is she going to play?
-I think she's going to go _____.
Great! Can I _____ too?

**Level THREE Unit FIFTEEN**
*Let's play games and sports!*

## Stay healthy!

Miss Patty says that when we play sports we keep our bodies healthy. Also, when we practice games our minds stay healthy too. So this week we are going to play sports and games. I am going to play checkers; I'm not going to play chess. Lucy and Michelle are going to play tag; they aren't going to jump rope. Tony and Harry are going to play football; they aren't going to play soccer. And Sandy isn't going to play volleyball; she's going to go swimming. As you can see we are going to have a healthy week, playing games and sports. What are you going to play? Stay healthy!

### What are they going to play?

1. What are you going to play?
   ❑ chess ❑ tag ❑ checkers
2. What are Lucy and Michelle going to play?
   ❑ tag ❑ jump rope ❑ swimming
3. What are Tony and Harry going to play?
   ❑ soccer ❑ volleyball ❑ football
4. What is Sandy going to play?
   ❑ volleyball ❑ swimming ❑ soccer

### Match 1-4 with a-d

1) Andy isn't going to play _____.
2) Lucy and Michelle aren't going to _____.
3) Tony and Harry aren't going to play _____.
4) Sandy isn't going to play _____.

# 15.4 Writing

Level THREE Unit FIFTEEN
*Let's play games and sports!*

Complete the reading with the words from the box below. Then read aloud.

### Stay healthy!

Miss Patty says that when we play sports we keep our bodies healthy. Also, when we practice games our minds stay healthy too. So this week we are going to play sports and games.
I am going to play _____; I'm not going to play _____.
Lucy and Michelle are going to play _____;
they aren't going to play _____.
Tony and Harry are going to play _____;
they aren't going to play _____.
And Sandy isn't going to play _____;
she's going to play _____.
As you can see we are going to have a healthy week, playing games and sports.
What are you going to play? I am going to play _____.
Stay healthy!

soccer • football • basketball • baseball • volley ball
swimming • chess • checkers • jump rope • tag

**Level THREE Unit FIFTEEN**
*Let's play games and sports!*

### FUTURE TENSE
We use BE + going to + verb
to express a planned action in the future.

We use WH - questions to ask for specific information.
Who = a person
What = a thing or action

We form WH question in the future tense;
Wh + be + subject + going to + verb + complement?

## Unscramble the sentences

1. ____ ____ ____ ____ ____ ?
is/ going to/ play/soccer/who

2. ____ ____ ____ ____ ____ ?
Sandy/ going to/is/what/play

3. ____ ____ ____ ____ ____ ?
Tony and Harry/ going to play/are/what

4. ____ ____ ____ ____ ____ ?
you/going to/ are/what /play

## Complete the answers

1. What are you going to play?
   -I ____ going to play ____.

2. What are you and Michelle going to play?
   -We ____ going to play ____.

3. What are Tony and Harry going to play?
   -They ____ going to play ____.

4. What is Sandy going to play?
   -She ____ going to play ____.

## How well did you do in this unit?
Write the CAN DO statement and assess yourself.
**Write 3, 2, or 1**
**3** = VERY WELL
**2** = WELL
**1** = NOT SO WELL

I CAN...
_____
_____
_____
_____
_____
_____
_____

**Level FOUR Unit ONE**
*Let's play with feelings!*

**16.1 Vocabulary**

## Learn the feelings

angry

cold

happy

hot

hungry

scared

sick

sleepy

thirsty

tired

## Unscramble the feelings words

1. yarng  _____
2. cdlo   _____
3. ayhpp  _____
4. yrgnhu _____
5. sdcrea _____
6. thtsyri _____

## 16.2 Dialogs

Level FOUR Unit ONE
Let's play with feelings!

### Practice the dialogs

Lucy looks angry.
-Yes, she is very angry!
I think she will shout aloud!
-OMG!

Tony looks happy.
-Yes, he is very happy!
I think he will sing.
-Great!

Lucy and Andy look tired.
-Yes, they are very tired!
I think they will go to sleep.
-That's good!

You look thirsty!
-Yes, we are very thirsty!
I think you will drink some water.
-Thank you!

You look hungry.
-Yes, I am very hungry!
I think you will eat a sandwich.
-Good idea!

You look _____.
-Yes, I am very _____!
I think you will _____.
-Good idea!

**Level FOUR Unit ONE**
*Let's play with feelings!*

16.3 Reading

## Feelings

We all have different feelings
and different ways to express them.
For example if Lucy is angry she will shout aloud.
But if Andy is angry, he will go away.
Let's see what our friends will do:
Tony is happy, he will sing.
Lucy and Andy are tired, they will sleep.
Sandy and Tony are thirsty, they will drink water.
Miss Patty is hungry, she will eat a sandwich.
I am scared I will cry; and if we are sick we will go to the doctor.
How do you feel today? What will you do?

## What will they do?

1. Lucy is angry she will _____
   ☐ cry  ☐ shout  ☐ sing
2. Tony is happy he will _____
   ☐ shout  ☐ cry  ☐ sing
3. Lucy and Andy are tired they will _____
   ☐ sleep  ☐ drink water  ☐ eat a sandwich
4. Sandy and Tony are thirsty they will _____
   ☐ drink water  ☐ eat a sandwich  ☐ go away
5. Miss Patty is hungry she will _____
   ☐ drink water  ☐ eat a sandwich  ☐ cry

## Match 1-5 with a-e

1. Lucy will shout if she's _____
2. Tony will sing if he's _____
3. Lucy and Andy will sleep if they're _____
4. Miss Patty will eat if she's _____
5. Sandy and Tony will drink water if they're _____

a   b   c

d   e

## 16.4 Writing

**Level FOUR Unit ONE**
*Let's play with feelings!*

Complete the reading with the words from the box below. Then read aloud.

### Feelings

We all have different feelings
and different ways to express them.
For example if Lucy is _____ she will _____.
But if Andy is _____, he will _____.
Let's see what our friends will do:
Tony is (1)_____, he will (2)_____.
Lucy and Andy are (1)_____, they will (2)_____.
Sandy and Tony are (1)_____, they will (2)_____.
Miss Patty is (1)_____, she will (2)_____.
I am (1) _____ I will (2)_____;
and we are (1) _____ we will (2)_____.
How do you feel today?
What will you do? I am _____ I will _____.

| 1 | angry • cold • happy • hot • hungry • scared<br>sick • sleepy • thirsty • tired |
|---|---|

| 2 | drink juice • drink water • eat • rest • shout • sleep<br>smile • tremble • visit a doctor • wear a sweater |
|---|---|

**Level FOUR Unit ONE**
*Let's play with feelings!*

### FUTURE TENSE WILL

We use WILL to express future events, with no plans or intentions: resolutions, promises, oaths, snap decisions, predictions

We make affirmative sentences in the future tense WILL:
Subject + WILL + base form of the verb
We can use any of the subjects with WILL:
I, you, he, she, it, we, they

Complete the sentences with the correct form of the verb WILL

1. Lucy is angry, she _____.
   • will shout    • will shouts    • will shouting

2. Tony is happy, he _____.
   • will smiling    • will going to smile    • will sing

3. I'm scared, I _____.
   • will going tremble    • will trembling    • will tremble

4. They're tired, they _____.
   • will go to sleep    • will going to sleep    • will sleeping

5. Miss Patty is hungry, she _____.
   • will eat    • will eating    • will eats

# How well did you do in this unit?
Write the CAN DO statement and assess yourself.
**Write 3, 2, or 1**
**3** = VERY WELL
**2** = WELL
**1** = NOT SO WELL

I CAN...
_____
_____
_____
_____
_____
_____
_____

**Level FOUR Unit TWO**
Let's play with time!

**17.1 Vocabulary**

## Learn the time expressions

IN (month) → August 2019 ← IN (year)

today → Thu 1
→ ON (day)

next week → 5 / 8

tomorrow ← Fri 2

next month → September 2019

AT (hour)

next year → August 2020

# 17.2 Dialogs

Level FOUR Unit TWO
Let's play with time!

## Practice the dialogs

Will you study English today?
-Yes, I will.
- I will have an exam tomorrow.

Will Sandy go to the movies next week?
-Yes, she will.
- She will go with her parents.

Will Tony play soccer on Sunday?
-Yes, he will.
- He will play with the school team.

Will you and your friends play baseball tomorrow at 6:00 o'clock?
-Yes, we will.
- We will play in the park

Will Lucy and Andy go to the zoo next month?
-Yes, they will.
- They will go to the zoo with their classmates.

Now you!

Will you _____ next _____?
-Yes, I will. I will _____.

## Level FOUR Unit TWO
*Let's play with time!*

**17.3 Reading**

### Very busy!

My friends and I will be very busy these days
we will do many interesting things.
Sandy will go to the movies with her parents next week.
Tony will play soccer on Sunday with the school team.
Lucy and Andy will go to the zoo next month
with their classmates.
My friends and I will play baseball tomorrow
at 6:00 o'clock in the park.
I will study English today, because
I will have an exam tomorrow in the morning.
Yes, we will be very busy these days.
Will you be busy?

### Answer true or false

1. Sandy will go to the park next week.
   True    False
2. Tony will play soccer on Saturday.
   True    False
3. Lucy and Andy will go to the zoo next month.
   True    False
4. My friends and I will play baseball tomorrow at 5 o'clock.
   True    False
5. I will study English today.
   True    False

### Who will…?

1. _____ will go to the movies with her parents next week.
2. _____ will play soccer on Sunday with the school team.
3. _____ will go to the zoo next month with their classmates.
4. _____ will play baseball tomorrow at 6:00 o'clock in the park.
5. _____ will study English today.

Lucy and Andy ◆ Sandy ◆ Tom
Tom and friends ◆ Tony

## 17.4 Writing

Level FOUR Unit TWO
Let's play with time!

Complete the reading with the words from the box below. Then read aloud.

**Very busy!**

My friends and I will be very busy these days
we will do many interesting things.
Sandy will go to the movies with her parents _____.
Tony will play soccer _____ with the school team.
Lucy and Andy will go to the zoo _____ with their classmates.
My friends and I will play baseball tomorrow
at _____ in the park.
I will study English today, because
I will have an exam _____ in the morning.
Yes, we will be very busy these days.
Will you be busy?
What will you do?
I will _____ _____.

next week • next month • next year tomorrow
at 6:00 o'clock (any time) • in August (any month)
on Saturday (any day of the week)

**Level FOUR Unit TWO**
*Let's play with time!*

**17.5**
Language in use

### FUTURE TENSE WILL

We use WILL to express future events.
with no plans or intentions:
resolutions, promises, oaths, snap decisions, predictions

We make interrogative sentences in the future tense WILL:
WILL + subject + base form of the verb + complement
Will Sandy go to the movies next week?
Short affirmative answer:
Yes, (comma) + personal pronoun + will. (period)
Yes, she will.

Read the questions and write a short affirmative answer

1. Will you study English today?
   -Yes, _____ _____.

2. Will Sandy go to the movies next week?
   -Yes, _____ _____.

3. Will Tony play soccer on Sunday?
   -Yes, _____ _____.

4. Will you and your friends play baseball tomorrow at 6:00 o'clock?
   -Yes, _____ _____.

5. Will Lucy and Andy go to the zoo next month?
   - Yes, _____ _____.

### Time to Rhyme!

A wise old owl sat in an oak,
The more he heard,
The less he spoke;
The less he spoke,
The more he heard;
Why can't we be
Like that wise old bird?

## How well did you do in this unit?

Write the CAN DO statement and assess yourself.

**Write 3, 2, or 1**

**3** = VERY WELL

**2** = WELL

**1** = NOT SO WELL

I CAN...

_____

_____

_____

_____

_____

_____

**Level FOUR. Unit THREE.**
*Let's play with transportation!*

18.1
Vocabulary

## Learn the means of transportation

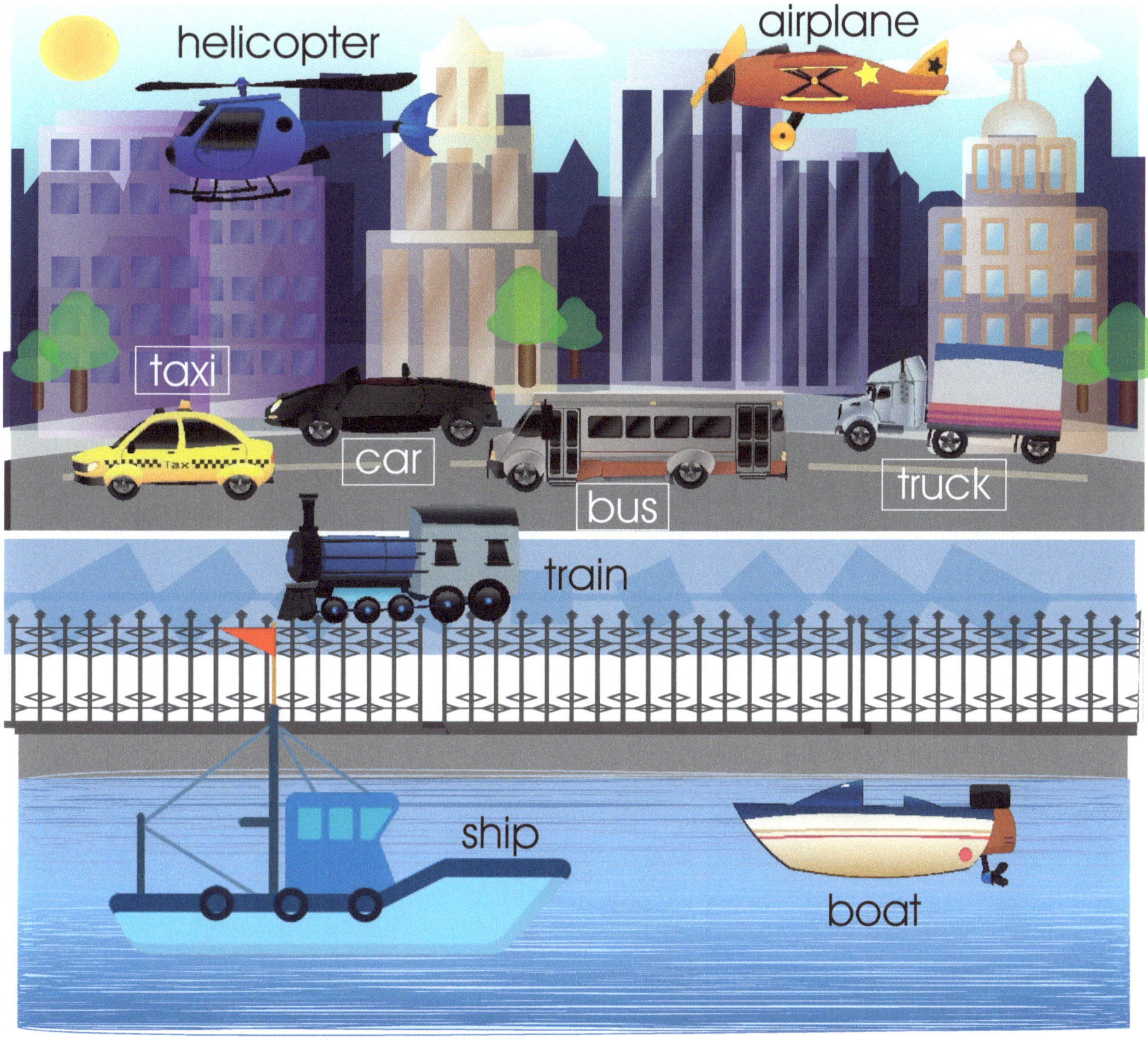

helicopter · airplane · taxi · car · bus · truck · train · ship · boat

## Find the transportation words

BUS     HELICOPTER
CAR     SHIP
TAXI    BOAT
TRAIN   TRUCK
AIRPLANE

| R | T | R | U | C | K | U | N | E | S |
|---|---|---|---|---|---|---|---|---|---|
| J | E | O | C | B | A | I | S | N | H |
| R | P | T | O | P | A | S | J | A | I |
| R | A | A | P | R | S | U | B | L | P |
| T | T | C | T | O | J | Y | L | P | Y |
| T | K | H | M | E | C | D | M | R | C |
| A | A | V | S | O | C | I | F | I | Z |
| W | G | X | Z | D | D | J | L | A | V |
| G | B | H | I | M | F | S | C | E | D |
| M | K | K | B | I | J | H | M | Z | H |

**18.2 Dialogs**

Level FOUR. Unit THREE.
Let's play with transportation!

Practice the dialogs

Will the bus arrive at 7:00 am?
-No, it won't arrive at 7:00 am.

Will the plane leave in the morning?
-No, it won't leave in the morning.

Will Sandy take the train on Sunday?
-No, she won't take the train on Sunday.

Will Tony ride in the boat next week?
-No, he won't ride in the boat next week.

Will Lucy get on the truck tomorrow?
-No, she won't get on the truck tomorrow.

*Now you!*

Will you _____ next _____?
-No, I won't _____.

**Level FOUR. Unit THREE.**
Let's play with transportation!

## WON'T, WON'T, WON'T!

Life is full of WONT'S!
Look: The plane WON'T leave in the morning
and the bus WON'T arrive at 7:00 o'clock;
Sandy WON'T take the train and Tony WON'T ride the boat;
Lucy WON'T get on the truck and Andy WON'T go to school by taxi!
So, what will happen? I think that the plane will leave in the afternoon
and the bus will arrive at 8:00 o'clock;
Sandy will take the taxi and Tony will ride in a ship;
Lucy will get on a helicopter and Andy will go to school by car.
Will all this happen? I don't know!
I think I will just have to wait and see!
WILL you or WON'T you?

According to the reading complete the sentences.

1. Tony _____ ride in a ship.
   ❑ will  ❑ won't
2. The plane _____ leave in the morning.
   ❑ will  ❑ won't
3. The bus _____ arrive at 7:00 o'clock.
   ❑ will  ❑ won't
4. Sandy _____ take the taxi.
   ❑ will  ❑ won't
5. Lucy _____ get on a helicopter.
   ❑ will  ❑ won't

Will they or won't they?

1. Will the plane leave in the morning?
   ❑ Yes, it will.  ❑ No, it won't.
2. Will Sandy take the taxi?
   ❑ Yes, she will.  ❑ No, she won't.
3. Will Tony ride in a boat?
   ❑ Yes, he will.  ❑ No, he won't.
4. Will Andy go to school by car?
   ❑ Yes, he will.  ❑ No, he won't.
5. Will Lucy get on a helicopter?
   ❑ Yes, she will.  ❑ No, she won't.

## 18.4 Writing

**Level FOUR. Unit THREE.**
*Let's play with transportation!*

Choose a word and fill in a blank. You can use WILL or WON'T as many times as you wish. Then read aloud.

> WON'T, WON'T, WON'T!
>
> Life is full of WONT's!
> Look: The plane _____ leave in the morning
> and the bus _____ arrive at 7:00 o'clock;
> Sandy _____ take the train and Tony _____ ride the boat;
> Lucy _____ get on the truck and Andy _____ go to school by taxi!
> So, what will happen? I think that the plane _____ leave
> in the afternoon and the bus _____ arrive at 8:00 o'clock;
> Sandy _____ take the taxi and Tony _____ ride in a ship;
> Lucy _____ get on a helicopter and Andy _____ go to school by car.
> Will all this happen? I don't know!
> I think I will just have to wait and see!
> WILL you or WON'T you?

WILL • WON'T

# 18.5 Language in use

## FUTURE TENSE WILL

We use WILL to express future events. with no plans or intentions: resolutions, promises, oaths, snap decisions, predictions

## FUTURE TENSE WILL

We use WILL to express future events.
We make negative sentences in the future tense WILL:
Subject +WILL+ NOT (WON'T) + base form of the verb + complement
Sandy WON'T take the train on Sunday.
They WON'T go to school by bus

### Unscramble the sentences

1. ___ ___ ___ ___ ___ ___.
   in / a / ship / Tony / ride / will

2. ___ ___ ___ ___ ___ ___.
   won't / the plane / in / the / leave / morning

3. ___ ___ ___ ___ ___ ___.
   at / 7:00 / the bus / arrive / won't / o'clock

4. ___ ___ ___ ___ ___.
   will / Lucy / get on / helicopter / a

5. ___ ___ ___ ___ ___ ___.
   won't / taxi / Andy / go to / by school

across

down

## How well did you do in this unit?
Write the CAN DO statement and assess yourself.
**Write 3, 2, or 1**
**3** = VERY WELL
**2** = WELL
**1** = NOT SO WELL

I CAN...
_____
_____
_____
_____
_____
_____
_____

**Level FOUR. Unit FOUR.**
*Let's play with the weather!*

## Learn the clothes and weather words

| | | | |
|---|---|---|---|
| hot | warm | cool | cold |
| sunny | cloudy | rainy | snowy |
| sunglasses | jeans | gloves | scarf |

**19.2 Dialogs**

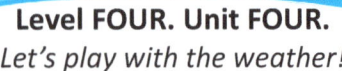

Level FOUR. Unit FOUR.
Let's play with the weather!

## Practice the dialogs

Will you wear a scarf tomorrow?
-No, I won't.
Why not?
-Because it will be hot tomorrow.

Will Lucy and Tony wear jeans tomorrow?
-Yes, they will.
Why?
-Because it will be cloudy tomorrow.

 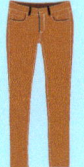

Will Tony wear sunglasses tomorrow?
-No, he won't.
Why not?
-Because it will be snowy tomorrow.

Will Andy wear gloves tomorrow?
-Yes, he will.
Why?
-Because it will be cool tomorrow.

Will Sandy wear jeans tomorrow?
-No, she won't.
Why not?
-Because it will be cold tomorrow..

Now you!

Will you _____ next _____?
-No, I won't _____.

Level FOUR. Unit FOUR.
Let's play with the weather!

## What to wear?

Do you know what you will wear when the weather is hot or cold?
Sunny or snowy? Well let me tell you!
Will it be sunny tomorrow?
Then, you will wear sunglasses,
you won't wear a scarf! Will it be snowy?
You will wear a scarf you won't wear sunglasses.
Will it be cloudy?
You will wear jeans, you won't wear gloves.
Will it be rainy?
You will wear gloves, you won't wear jeans.
You see! What you will wear tomorrow will depend on the weather!
What will you wear tomorrow?

According to the reading complete the sentences

1. I won't wear a _____ tomorrow, because it will be hot.

2. We will wear sunglasses tomorrow because it will be _____.

3. Sandy won't wear _____ tomorrow because it will be cold.

4. Andy will wear gloves tomorrow because it will be _____.

5. Tony won't wear _____ tomorrow because it will be snowy.

What will you wear tomorrow?

1. It will be sunny tomorrow;
   you won't wear:
   ❑ sunglasses  ❑ scarf  ❑ jeans

2. It will be snowy tomorrow;
   you will wear:
   ❑ scarf  ❑ sunglasses  ❑ jeans

3. It will be cloudy tomorrow;
   you won't wear:
   ❑ jeans  ❑ gloves  ❑ scarf

4. It will be rainy tomorrow;
   you will wear:
   ❑ jeans  ❑ sunglasses  ❑ gloves

## 19.4 Writing

**Level FOUR. Unit FOUR.**
*Let's play with the weather!*

Choose a word and fill in a blank. You can use the clothes as many times as you wish. Then read aloud.

### What to wear?

Do you know what you will wear when the weather is hot or cold?
Sunny or snowy? Well let me tell you!
Will it be sunny tomorrow?
Then, you will wear _____, you won't wear a _____!
Will it be snowy? You will wear a _____ you won't wear _____.
Will it be cloudy? You will wear _____, you won't wear ____.
Will it be rainy? You will wear _____, you won't wear _____.
You see! What you will wear tomorrow will depend on the weather!
What will you wear tomorrow? –I will wear_____

**sunglasses • jeans • gloves • scarf**

**Level FOUR. Unit FOUR.**
*Let's play with the weather!*

## FUTURE TENSE WILL

We use WILL to express future events with no plans or intentions: resolutions, promises, oaths, snap decisions, predictions

We make short affirmative answers:
Yes, (comma) + personal pronoun + WILL. (period)
Yes, she will.
We make short negative answers:
No, (comma) + personal pronoun + WILL. (period)
No, they won't.

### Write the correct short answer

1. Will you wear a scarf tomorrow?
   _____

2. Will Tony wear sunglasses tomorrow?
   _____

3. Will Lucy and Andy wear jeans tomorrow?
   _____

4. Will Sandy wear gloves tomorrow?
   _____

### Choose the correct option

1. Which is correct?
   ❑ Yes, I will.
   ❑ Yes I will
   ❑ Yes I will.

2. Which is correct?
   ❑ No they won't
   ❑ No, they won't
   ❑ No, they won't.

3. Which is correct?
   ❑ Yes, she will
   ❑ Yes, she will.
   ❑ Yes she will

4. Which is correct?
   ❑ No, we won't.
   ❑ No we won't
   ❑ No we won't.

## How well did you do in this unit?
Write the CAN DO statement and assess yourself.
**Write 3, 2, or 1**
**3** = VERY WELL
**2** = WELL
**1** = NOT SO WELL

I CAN...
_____
_____
_____
_____
_____
_____

**Level FOUR. Unit FIVE.**
*Let's play with after school!*

**20.1** Vocabulary

## Learn the after school and vacation activities

### leisure activities

watch TV

listen to music

read books

play cards

play video games

go to the movies

### vacation activities

go hiking

go swimming

go camping

go fishing

## 20.2 Dialogs

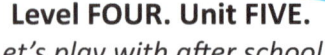

**Level FOUR. Unit FIVE.**
*Let's play with after school!*

### Practice the dialogs

What will you do on the weekend?
-I think I will go to movies or maybe I will play video games.
I really can't decide.

What will you do in the summer?
-I think I will go swimming or maybe I will go hiking.
 really can't decide.

What will you do after school?
-I think I will watch TV or maybe I will listen to music.
I really can't decide.

What will you do on vacation?
-I think I will go fishing or maybe I will go camping.
I really can't decide.

What will you do on Saturday?
-I think I will read books or maybe I will play cards.
I really can't decide.

*Now you!*

What will you do on _____?
-I think I will _____ or maybe
I will _____.
I really can't decide.

**Level FOUR. Unit FIVE.**
*Let's play with after school!*

**20.3** Reading

## I really can't decide!

There are so many fun activities for after school, on vacation, in the summer; that I really can't decide what to do! My friends can't decide either.
Andy thinks he will go swimming or maybe he will go hiking in the summer; he really can't decide!
Tony thinks he will go fishing or maybe he will go camping on vacation; he really can't decide!
Sandy thinks she will go to the movies or maybe she will play video games on the weekend; she really can't decide.
Lucy thinks she will watch TV or maybe she will listen to music after school; she really can't decide.
Harry thinks he will read books or maybe he will play cards on Saturday; he really can't decide.
And me, what will I do?
I really can't decide! What will you do? Can you decide?

**Read and answer true or false according to the reading**

1. Maybe Harry will read books.
   ☐ True    ☐ False
2. Maybe Lucy will go swimming.
   ☐ True    ☐ False
3. Maybe Sandy will go to the movies.
   ☐ True    ☐ False
4. Maybe Tony will go fishing.
   ☐ True    ☐ False
5. Maybe Andy will play cards.
   ☐ True    ☐ False

**According to the reading which is CORRECT which is INCORRECT?**
✓    ✗

1. Andy thinks he will go swimming.
   ✓    ✗
2. Tony thinks he will go to the movies.
   ✓    ✗
3. Sandy thinks she will play video games.
   ✓    ✗
4. Lucy thinks she will read books.
   ✓    ✗
5. Harry thinks he will play cards.
   ✓    ✗

## 20.4 Writing

**Level FOUR. Unit FIVE.**
*Let's play with after school!*

Choose a word and fill in a blank. You can use the activities as many times as you wish. Then read aloud.

### I really can't decide!

There are so many fun activities for after school, on vacation, in the summer; that I really can't decide what to do! My friends can't decide either.
Andy thinks he will _____ or maybe he will _____ in the summer; he really can't decide! Tony thinks he will _____ or maybe he will _____ on vacation; he really can't decide! Sandy thinks she will _____ or maybe she will _____ on the weekend; she really can't decide. Lucy thinks she will _____ or maybe she will _____ after school; she really can't decide. Harry thinks he will _____ or maybe he will _____ on Saturday; he really can't decide. And me, what will I do? I really can't decide! What will you do? I think I will _____ or maybe I will _____?

watch TV • listen to music • read books • play cards
play video games • go to the movies • go hiking
go swimming • go camping • go fishing

**Level FOUR. Unit FIVE.**
Let's play with after school!

**20.5 Language in use**

## FUTURE TENSE WILL

We use WILL to express future events
with no plans or intentions:
resolutions, promises, oaths, snap decisions, predictions

We form WH- questions with WILL:
WH + will + subject + verb + complement.
What will you do on Saturday?
I will go to the movies.

## Choose the correct question

1. Which is correct?
   ☐ What will you do?
   ☐ What will you does?
2. Which is correct?
   ☐ Where you will go?
   ☐ Where will you go?
3. Which is correct?
   ☐ When will he studies?
   ☐ When will he study?
4. Which is correct?
   ☐ Who you will invite?
   ☐ Who will you invite?
5. Which is correct?
   ☐ What will I eat?
   ☐ What I will eat?

## Time to Rhyme!

What are little girls made of?
Sugar and spice,
And everything nice.
That's what little girls are made of.
What are little boys made of?
Snips and snails,
And puppy dogs' tails.
That's what little boys are made of.

# How well did you do in this unit?
Write the CAN DO statement and assess yourself.
**Write 3, 2, or 1**
**3** = VERY WELL
**2** = WELL
**1** = NOT SO WELL

I CAN...
_____
_____
_____
_____
_____
_____
_____

**Level FOUR. Unit SIX.**
*Let's play with school supplies!*

**21.1 Vocabulary**

# Learn the school supplies words

scissors

school bag

glue stick

pencil case

marker

sharpener

lunch box

ruler

book

notebook

## Unscramble the words

kobo _____

rrkmae _____

ntbkoooe _____

lrreu _____

ssssrcoi _____

eearnprhs _____

## 21.2 Dialogs

**Level FOUR. Unit SIX.**
Let's play with school supplies!

### Practice the dialogs

Is this your schoolbag?
-No, it isn't.
-That is Sandy's schoolbag.

Are these your markers?
-No, they aren't.
-Those are Andy's markers.

Is this your sharpener?
-No, it isn't.
-That is Lucy's sharpener.

Are these your rulers?
-No, they aren't.
-Those are Tony's rulers.

Is this your lunch box?
-No, it isn't.
-That is Andy's lunch box.

Now you!

Are these your _____?
-No, they aren't. Those are _____ _____.

Is this your _____?
-No, it isn't. That is _____ _____.

**Level FOUR. Unit SIX.**
*Let's play with school supplies!*

## Clean up time!

It's clean up time at school.
There are many things out of place in our classroom
and Miss Patty wants to know who all those things belong to.
Whose schoolbag is this? She asks;
that is Sandy's schoolbag! I will get it Miss Patty, Sandy says.
And whose scissors are these? Those are Tony's scissors!
Thank you, says Tony.
And this sharpener, whose is it? That's my sharpener.
Oh! I really need that sharpener, thanks.
Come and look under the desk.
Those are Andy's markers. Oh, sorry! Says Andy.
Sandy's lunch box is near the door;
and Tony's rulers are on the floor! What a mess!
Well clean up time is done and we all have our things back.
Our classroom is clean!
Until next clean up time!

### Read and answer true or false according to the reading

1. That is Sandy's school bag.
   ☐ True   ☐ False

2. Those are Andy's scissors.
   ☐ True   ☐ False

3. That's Lucy's sharpener.
   ☐ True   ☐ False

4. Those are Tony's markers.
   ☐ True   ☐ False

5. That is Lucy's lunch box.
   ☐ True   ☐ False

6. Those are Tony's rulers.
   ☐ True   ☐ False

### Complete the answers according to the reading

1. Is this your schoolbag?
   -No, it isn't.
   -That's _____ schoolbag.

2. Are these your scissors?
   -No, they aren't.
   -Those are _____ scissors.

3. Are these your markers?
   -No, they aren't.
   -Those are _____ markers.

4. Is this your lunch box?
   -No, it isn't.
   -That's _____ lunch box.

5. Are these your rulers?
   -No, they aren't.
   -Those are _____ rulers.

## 21.4 Writing

**Level FOUR. Unit SIX.**
*Let's play with school supplies!*

Choose a word and fill in a blank. You can use the names as many times as you wish. Then read aloud.

### Clean up time!

It's clean up time at school.
There are many things out of place in our classroom;
and Miss Patty wants to know who all those things belong to.
Whose schoolbag is this? She asks; that is _____ schoolbag!
And whose scissors are these? Those are _____ scissors!
And this sharpener, whose is it? That's _____ sharpener.
Oh! I really need that sharpener, thanks.
Come and look under the desk.
Those are _____ markers. _____ lunch box is near the door;
and _____ rulers are on the floor! What a mess!
Well clean up time is done and we all have our things back.
Our classroom is neat!
Until next clean up time!

Andy • Tony • Lucy • Sandy

**Level FOUR. Unit SIX.**
*Let's play with school supplies!*

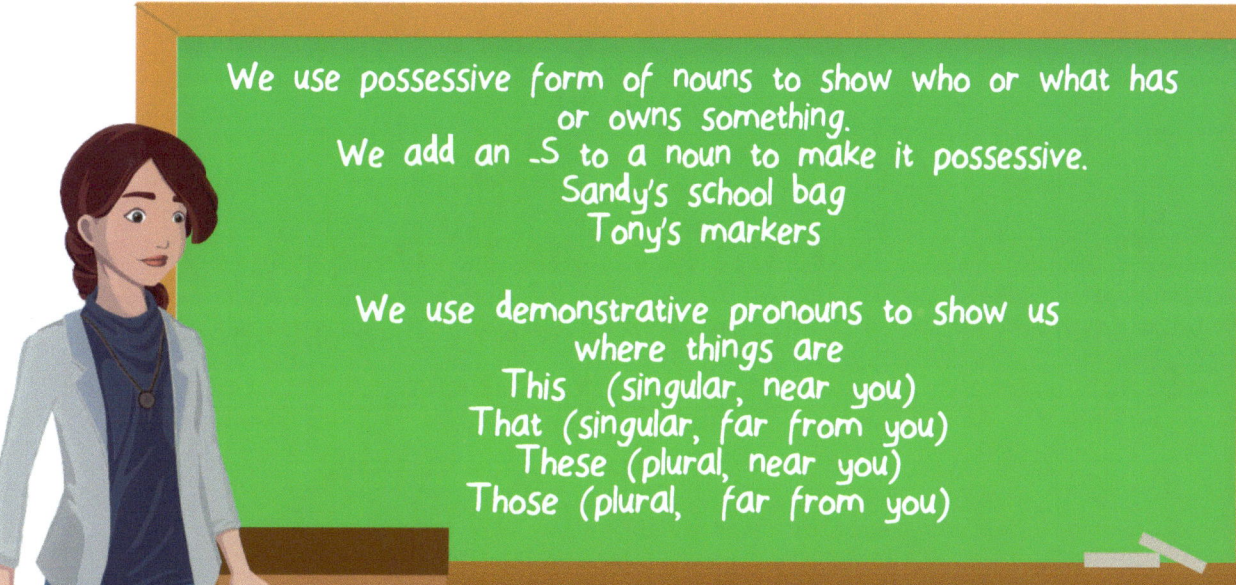

Read carefully. Choose the correct phrase.

1. Which is correct?
   - ☐ Sandy's notebook
   - ☐ Sandys notebook
2. Which is correct?
   - ☐ Tonys' markers
   - ☐ Tony's markers
3. Which is correct?
   - ☐ Lucy's sharpeners
   - ☐ Lucys' sharpeners
4. Which is correct?
   - ☐ Andys pencil case
   - ☐ Andy's pencil case
5. Which is correct?
   - ☐ That is Tony's books
   - ☐ Those are Tony's books
6. Which is correct?
   - ☐ This is Lucy's glue stick
   - ☐ These are Lucy's glue stick
7. Which is correct?
   - ☐ That is Sandy's notebook
   - ☐ Those are Sandy's notebook
8. Which is correct?
   - ☐ This is Andy's ruler
   - ☐ This is Andy's rulers

**How well did you do in this unit?**
Write the CAN DO statement and assess yourself.
**Write 3, 2, or 1**
**3** = VERY WELL
**2** = WELL
**1** = NOT SO WELL

I CAN...
_____
_____
_____
_____
_____
_____
_____

**Level FOUR. Unit SEVEN.**
*Let's play with school illnesses!*

**22.1 Vocabulary**

Learn the illnesses words

backache        earache        fever        headache

stomachache    sore throat    toothache    cold

Unscramble the words

bckchaae         _____
eaaehcr          _____
aehtcomahcs      _____
thoacohet        _____
revef            _____

135

## 22.2 Dialogs

**Level FOUR. Unit SEVEN.**
Let's play with school illnesses!

### Practice the dialogs

How do you feel today?
-Not so good.
What's wrong?
-I have a headache.
I'm sorry to hear that.

How are you?
-Not very well.
What's the matter?
-I have an earache.
I'm sorry to hear that.

How are you today?
-I'm sick.
What's the matter?
-I have a stomachache.
I'm sorry to hear that.

How are you today?
-I'm sick.
What's the matter?
-I have a fever.
I'm sorry to hear that.

How do you feel?
-I feel sick.
What's wrong?
-I have a toothache.
I'm sorry to hear that.

How do you feel?
-I feel sick/ Not very well/ I'm sick/Not so good
What's wrong?
-I have _____.
I'm sorry to hear that.

**Level FOUR. Unit SEVEN.**
Let's play with school illnesses!

### Everybody is sick today

It is not a good day today at school.
Everybody feels sick today!
What's the matter with everybody?
Sandy doesn't feel well; she has a terrible earache
and a sore throat.
Lucy is not feeling good today; she has a headache.
Andy is feeling sick today; he has a fever and a stomachache.
Tony is not very well; he has a cold.
Tom doesn't feel well; he has a toothache.
Even Miss Patty doesn't feel well; she has a terrible backache!
I am very sorry to hear that everybody is sick today.
It sure isn't a good day at school today!
How do you feel today?

According to the reading choose the correct answer

1. Sandy has a _____ today.
   ❑ sore throat  ❑ cold  ❑ fever
2. Andy has a _____ today.
   ❑ sore throat  ❑ cold  ❑ fever
3. Tony has _____ today.
   ❑ sore throat  ❑ cold  ❑ fever
4. Lucy has a _____ today.
   ❑ headache  ❑ backache
   ❑ toothache
5. Miss Patty has a _____ today.
   ❑ headache  ❑ backache
   ❑ toothache

Who is sick?

1. Who has a toothache?
   ❑ Lucy  ❑ Miss Patty  ❑ Tom
2. Who has a backache?
   ❑ Sandy  ❑ Tom  ❑ Miss Patty
3. Who has a headache?
   ❑ Lucy  ❑ Andy  ❑ Tony
4. Who has a cold?
   ❑ Tony  ❑ Andy  ❑ Tom
5. Who has a stomachache?
   ❑ Lucy  ❑ Tom  ❑ Andy
6. Who has an earache?
   ❑ Tom  ❑ Sandy  ❑ Andy

**Level FOUR. Unit SEVEN.**
*Let's play with school illnesses!*

Choose a word and fill in a blank. You can use the illnesses as many times as you wish. Then read aloud.

Everybody is sick today

It is not a good day today at school.
Everybody feels sick today! What's the matter with everybody?
Sandy doesn't feel well; she has a terrible _____ and a _____ .
Lucy is not feeling good today; she has a _____ .
Andy is feeling sick today; he has a _____ and a _____ .
Tony is not very well; he has a _____ .
Tom doesn't feel well; he has a _____ .
Even Miss Patty doesn't feel well; she has a terrible _____ !
I am very sorry to hear that everybody is sick today.
It sure isn't a good day at school today!
How do you feel today?

backache • cold • earache • fever • headache
sore throat • stomachache • toothache

**Level FOUR. Unit SEVEN.**
*Let's play with school illnesses!*

- How do you feel today?
- I'm fine, thank you!
  Great!
  Good!
  Fantastic!
  I'm glad to hear that!

- How do you feel?
- I'm sick
- I feel sick.
- Not so good.
- Not very well.
- I'm sorry to hear that!

## Find the illnesses

BACKACHE
EARACHE
FEVER
HEADACHE
SORE THROAT
STOMACHACHE
TOOTHACHE
COLD

| V | E | B | E | R | M | S | E | A | L |
|---|---|---|---|---|---|---|---|---|---|
| O | H | T | H | M | L | E | A | L | L |
| J | B | E | C | Y | D | Y | R | O | B |
| J | Z | R | A | I | Z | T | A | O | D |
| M | J | R | H | D | H | Q | C | D | S |
| K | R | T | T | R | A | B | H | L | R |
| M | V | Q | O | T | E | C | E | O | I |
| N | E | A | O | U | T | L | H | C | V |
| T | T | M | T | R | R | E | V | E | F |
| B | A | C | K | A | C | H | E | A | V |

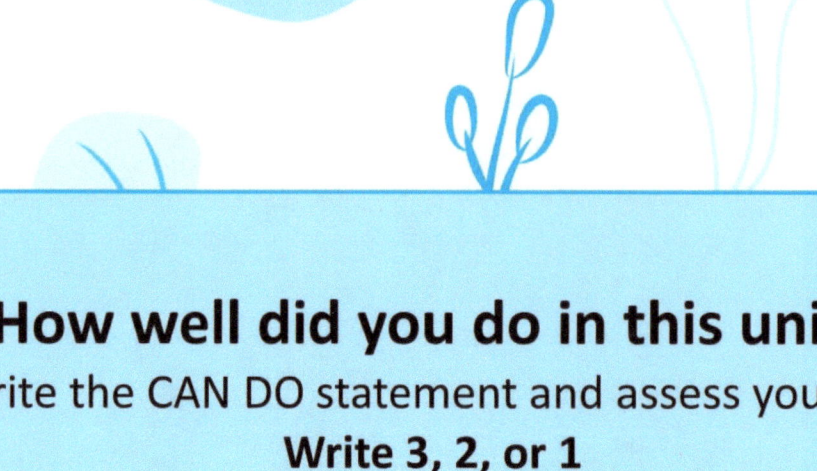

**How well did you do in this unit?**
Write the CAN DO statement and assess yourself.
**Write 3, 2, or 1**
**3** = VERY WELL
**2** = WELL
**1** = NOT SO WELL

I CAN...
_____
_____
_____
_____
_____
_____
_____

**Level FOUR. Unit EIGHT.**
*Let's play with irregular plurals!*

**23.1** Vocabulary

## Learn the irregular plurals

mouse — mice

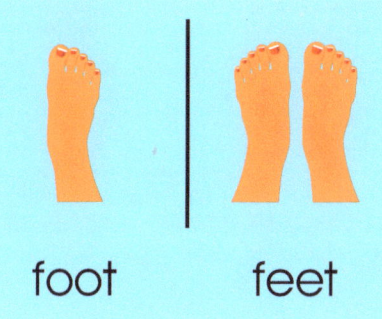
foot — feet

fish — fish

child — children

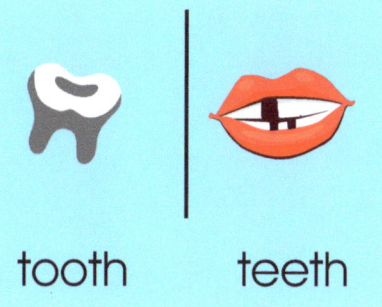
tooth — teeth

deer — deer

man — men

sheep — sheep

goose — geese

## Write the plural of the following nouns

woman — women

| | | | |
|---|---|---|---|
| child | _____ | man | _____ |
| deer | _____ | mouse | _____ |
| fish | _____ | sheep | _____ |
| foot | _____ | tooth | _____ |
| goose | _____ | woman | _____ |

## 23.2 Dialogs

**Level FOUR. Unit EIGHT.**
*Let's play with irregular plurals!*

Practice the dialogs

What is the plural of MAN?
-The plural of man is MEN.
How do you spell it?
-M-E-N
Thank you.
-You're welcome!

What is the plural of TOOTH?
-The plural of tooth is TEETH.
How do you spell it?
-T-E-E-T-H
Thank you.
-You're welcome!

What is the plural of CHILD?
-The plural of child is CHILDREN.
How do you spell it?
-C-H-I-L-D-R-E-N
Thank you.
-You're welcome!

What is the plural of WOMAN?
-The plural of woman is WOMEN.
How do you spell it?
-W-O-M-E-N
Thank you.
-You're welcome!

What is the plural of _____?
-The plural of _____ is _____.
How do you spell it?
-_____
Thank you.
-You're welcome!

*Now you!*

Level FOUR. Unit EIGHT.
*Let's play with irregular plurals!*

**23.3 Reading**

## Three mice

I can't believe what I am seeing!
Three mice with glasses!
No, wait…! I see three mice turning into three men with glasses;
They are going into the dentist's office and he is pulling out
three front teeth! I can't believe what I am seeing!
Three women across the street see them and run away
because they have no teeth! I can't believe what I am seeing!
Those three mice that turned into three men are now three fish,
three feet long each! I can't believe what I am seeing!
The three feet long fish are turning into three children
with three geese each! I can't believe what I am seeing!
I can't believe what I am seeing… because my friend is waking me up.
I am in the middle of my English class!
Sorry Miss Patty, what are you explaining? Oh yes, irregular plurals!
Can you believe what you are reading?

Complete the sentences with the correct irregular plural noun?

According to the story answer true or false.

*He can't believe what he is seeing:*

1. Three _____ with glasses.

2. Three mice turning into three _____ with glasses.

3. The dentist is pulling out three front _____ .

4. Three _____ are running away.

5. Three men turning into three _____ .

6. Three fish are turning into three _____ with three _____ .

1. Three mice are turning into fish.
   ❏ True   ❏ False

2. Three men are running.
   ❏ True   ❏ False

3. The fish are three feet long.
   ❏ True   ❏ False

4. The dentist is pulling three front teeth.
   ❏ True   ❏ False

5. Three children have three mice.
   ❏ True   ❏ False

## 23.4 Writing

**Level FOUR. Unit EIGHT.**
*Let's play with irregular plurals!*

Choose a word and fill in a blank. You can use the nouns as many times as you wish. Then read aloud.

### Three mice

I can't believe what I am seeing!
Three _____ with glasses! No, wait…! I see three _____ turning into three _____ with glasses; They are going into the dentist's office and he is pulling out three front _____!
I can't believe what I am seeing!
Three _____ across the street see them and run away because they have no _____! I can't believe what I am seeing!
Those three _____ that turned into three _____ are now three _____, three feet long each!
I can't believe what I am seeing!
The three feet long _____ are turning into three _____ with three _____ each! I can't believe what I am seeing!
I can't believe what I am seeing… because my friend is waking me up.
I am in the middle of my English class!
Sorry Miss Patty! What are you explaining? Oh yes, irregular plurals!
Can you believe what you are reading?

mice • teeth • feet • children • men • women
fish • deer • sheep • geese

**Level FOUR. Unit EIGHT.**
*Let's play with irregular plurals!*

### Irregular Plural Nouns
We make most nouns plural by adding "s" or "es" to the end of the word.
book = books            glass = glasses

But there are some nouns that don't follow the rules. They are called irregular nouns because they don't become plural the "regular" way.

mouse – mice          woman – women
tooth – teeth         goose – geese
foot – feet           fish – fish
child – children      deer – deer
man – men             sheep – sheep

## Choose the correct sentence

1. Which is correct?
   ☐ Those womans are nice.
   ☐ Those women are nice.
2. Which is correct?
   ☐ There are three mice.
   ☐ There are three mouses.
3. Which is correct?
   ☐ The boy is four feet tall.
   ☐ The boy is four foots tall.
4. Which is correct?
   ☐ My front tooths are missing.
   ☐ My front teeth are missing.
5. Which is correct?
   ☐ The childrens are playing.
   ☐ The children are playing.
6. Which is correct?
   ☐ I see three mens with glasses.
   ☐ I see three men with glasses.

## Match the singular with the plural form of the nouns

a) child    (___) mice
b) deer     (___) teeth
c) fish     (___) feet
d) foot     (___) children
e) goose    (___) men
f) man      (___) women
g) mouse    (___) fish
h) sheep    (___) deer
l) tooth    (___) sheep
j) woman    (___) geese

# How well did you do in this unit?
Write the CAN DO statement and assess yourself.
**Write 3, 2, or 1**
**3** = VERY WELL
**2** = WELL
**1** = NOT SO WELL

I CAN...
_____
_____
_____
_____
_____
_____
_____

**Level FOUR. Unit NINE.**
*Let's play with home!*

## Learn the furniture in the home

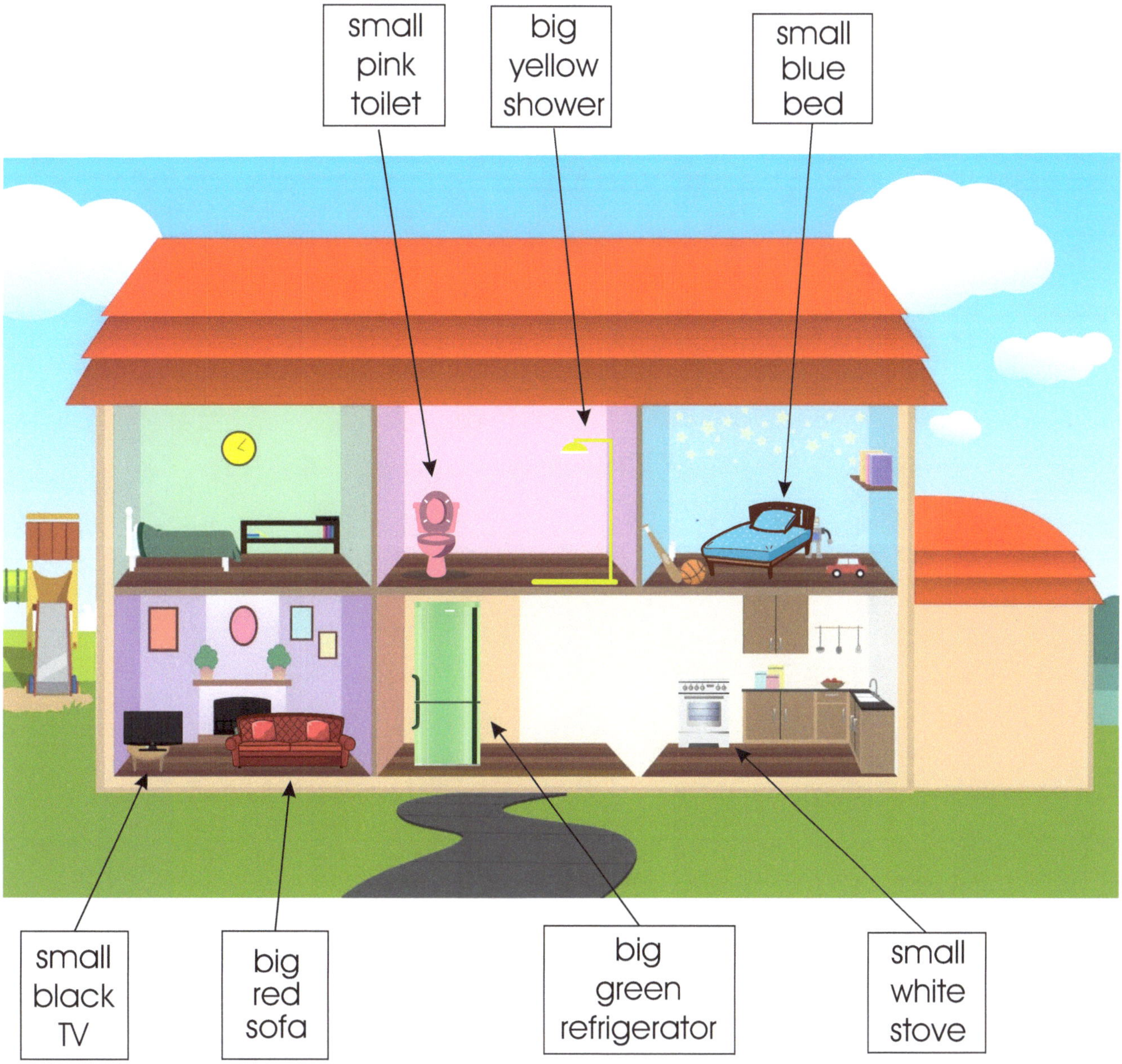

- small pink toilet
- big yellow shower
- small blue bed
- small black TV
- big red sofa
- big green refrigerator
- small white stove

**24.2 Dialogs**

Level FOUR. Unit NINE.
Let's play with home!

## Practice the dialogs

What is there in your living room?
-There is a big red sofa.
Really?
-Yes, there is. It is very big.

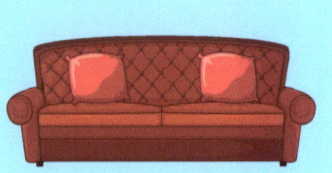

What is there in your kitchen?
-There is a small white stove.
Really?
-Yes, there is. It is very small.

What is there in your bedroom?
-There is small blue bed.
Really?
-Yes, there is. It is very small.

What is there in your kitchen?
-There is a big green refrigerator.
Really?
-Yes, there is. It is very big.

What is there in your living room?
-There is small black TV.
Really?
-Yes, there is. It is very small.

What is there in your bathroom?
-There is a big yellow shower.
Really?
-Yes, there is. It is very big.

What is there in your _____?
-There is a big/ small _____ _____.
Really?
-Yes, there is. It is very big/small.

Now you!

**Level FOUR. Unit NINE.**
Let's play with home!

## My favorite place at home

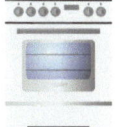

I live in a beautiful home.
There are many things inside.
There is a big red sofa and
there is a small black TV in the living room.
There is a small white stove and
there is a big green refrigerator in the kitchen.
There is a small yellow shower and
there is a big pink toilet in the bathroom.
There are two beds in my bedroom one
for my brother and there is one for me, a small blue bed.
And of all the things there are at home,
my favorite place is my small blue bed, I just love it!
What is your favorite place at home?

### Answer the questions according to the reading

1. What is there in the kitchen?
   - A small green refrigerator
   - A big green refrigerator
   - A small white refrigerator
2. What is there in the living room?
   - A big red sofa
   - A small red sofa
   - A small black sofa
3. What is there in the bathroom?
   - A small pink toilet
   - A big pink toilet
   - A small pink shower
4. What is there in the bedroom?
   - A big blue bed
   - A big red bed
   - A small blue bed

### According to the story answer circle true or false

1. There is a small red bed in the bedroom.
   True    False
2. There is a big green refrigerator in the kitchen.
   True    False
3. There is a big black TV in the living room.
   True    False
4. There is small red sofa in the living room.
   True    False
5. There is a small white stove in the kitchen.
   True    False

## 24.4 Writing

**Level FOUR. Unit NINE.**
*Let's play with home!*

Choose a word and fill in a blank. You can use sizes and colors as many times as you wish. Then read aloud.

### My favorite place at home

I live in a beautiful home. There are many things inside.
There is a _____ _____ sofa and
there is a _____ _____ TV in the living room.
There is a _____ _____ stove and
there is a _____ _____ refrigerator in the kitchen.
There is a _____ _____ shower and
there is a _____ _____ toilet in the bathroom.
There are two beds in my bedroom
one for my brother and there is one for me, a _____ _____ bed.
And of all the things there are at home,
my favorite place is my _____ _____ bed, I just love it!
What is your favorite place at home?

small • big • red • white • blue • black
green • yellow • pink

 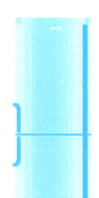 

**Level FOUR. Unit NINE.**
*Let's play with home!*

### There is - There are
We use there is /there are to express that something exists (or does not exist)

**Affirmative:**
Singular - There is a white stove in the kitchen.
Plural - There are two beds in the bedroom.

**Negative:**
Singular - There isn't a big stove in the kitchen.
Plural - There aren't two big beds in the bedroom.

**Interrogative:**
Singular - Is there a big bed in the bedroom?
Plural - Are there two sofas in the living room?

### Order of Adjectives
When we have two adjectives + a noun,
the adjectives must follow a specific order.
size + color + noun
a big (size) red (color) sofa (noun)

## Choose the correct sentence

1. Which is correct?
   - A red big bed
   - A big red bed
2. Which is correct?
   - A blue small sofa
   - A small blue sofa
3. Which is correct?
   - There is two beds in the bedroom
   - There are two beds in the bedroom
4. Which is correct?
   - There isn't a yellow shower
   - There aren't a yellow shower

## Unscramble the sentences

1. ____ ____ ____ ____ ____ ____ .
   blue / there / big / is / a / bed

2. ____ ____ ____ ____ ____ .
   sofas / red / big / are / there

3. ____ ____ ____ ____ ____ ____ ?
   TV / is / black / there / small / a

4. ____ ____ ____ ____ ____ ____ .
   a / toilet / there / small / isn't / pink

## How well did you do in this unit?

Write the CAN DO statement and assess yourself.
**Write 3, 2, or 1**
**3** = VERY WELL
**2** = WELL
**1** = NOT SO WELL

I CAN...
_____
_____
_____
_____
_____
_____
_____

**Level FOUR. Unit TEN.**
*Let's play in our free time!*

**25.1 Vocabulary**

## Learn the free time activities

computer games

watch TV

read books

go to the movies

go hiking

go swimming

soccer

jogging

## Complete the free time activities

1. c _ _ _ _ _ _ _ r   g _ _ _ _
2. r _ _ _   b _ _ _ s
3. j _ _ _ _ _ g
4. s _ _ _ _ r
5. w _ _ _ _ TV

### 25.2 Dialogs

**Level FOUR. Unit TEN.**
*Let's play in our free time!*

## Practice the dialogs

Do you like soccer?
-No, I don't like it.
Why not?
-I think it's boring!
No, it isn't. I like it very much.
-Well, I don't.

Do you like computer games?
-Yes, I like them.
Why?
-I think they are very exciting!
No, they aren't. I don't like them at all.
-Well, I do.

Do you like to read Fairy Tales?
-Yes, I like them.
Why?
-I think they are very exciting!
No, they aren't. I don't like them at all.
-Well, I do.

Do you like swimming?
-No, I don't like it.
Why not?
-I think it's boring!
No, it isn't. I like it very much.
-Well, I don't.

Now you!

Do you like _____?
-No, I don't like it/them.
Why not?
-I think _____!
No, it isn't. /No, they aren't. I like it/them very much.
-Well, I don't.

**Level FOUR. Unit TEN.**
*Let's play in our free time!*

25.3 Reading

## What do you like?

My friends and I all like to do different activities after school; but we don't like the same things.
I like soccer and Andy doesn't like it at all; he thinks it's boring.
Tony likes to play computer games he thinks they are exciting but Lucy doesn't like them at all.
Andy likes to go jogging in the park but Tony doesn't like it at all; he thinks it's boring.
Lucy doesn't like to read fairy tales, and I like them very much; I think they are very interesting.
Tony doesn't like to go swimming but Lucy likes it very much.
Even though my friends and I like different things, we are all good friends.
What do you and your friends like to do after school?

**Choose what they like to do after school**

1. What does Sandy like?
   ❑ soccer   ❑ computer games
   ❑ swimming
2. What does Lucy like?
   ❑ soccer   ❑ swimming
   ❑ computer games
3. What does Tony like?
   ❑ computer games   ❑ soccer
   ❑ swimming
4. What does Andy like?
   ❑ soccer   ❑ jogging
   ❑ read books
5. What doesn't Lucy like?
   ❑ computer games   ❑ swimming
   ❑ jogging

**Answer according to the reading. Circle ✓ if yes. Circle ✗ if no.**

1. Who likes to play computer games?
   Lucy          Tony

2. Who likes jogging?
   Andy          Tony

3. Who likes to read?
   Lucy          Sandy

4. Who likes swimming?
   Lucy          Tony

155

## 25.4 Writing

**Level FOUR. Unit TEN.**
*Let's play in our free time!*

Choose a word and fill in a blank. You can use the free time activities as many times as you wish. Then read aloud.

### What do you like?

My friends and I all like to do different activities after school;
but we don't like the same things.
I like _____ and Andy doesn't like it at all.
Tony likes _____ he thinks it is exciting
but Lucy doesn't like it at all.
Andy likes _____ but Tony doesn't like it at all.
Lucy doesn't like _____, and I like it very much.
Tony doesn't like _____ but Lucy likes it very much.
Even though my friends and I like different things,
we are all good friends.
What do you and your friends like to do after school?
I like _____ and my friends like _____ .

---

to play computer games • to watch TV • to read books
to go to the movies • hiking • swimming
soccer • jogging

---

**Level FOUR. Unit TEN.**
*Let's play in our free time!*

**OBJECT PRONOUNS**
The seven basic pronouns have one form when they are used as subjects and another form when they are used as objects. Subject pronouns do the action. Objects pronouns receive the action.

| Subject Pronoun | OBJECT PRONOUN |
|---|---|
| I | ME |
| You | YOU |
| He | HIM |
| She | HER |
| It | IT |
| We | US |
| They | THEM |

Write the OBJECT PRONOUN

1. I play with _____ (Tony) after school.

2. My dad reads books to _____ (I).

3. She talks to _____ (Sandy and Lucy) every day.

4. We go with _____ (Lucy) to school.

5. They go swimming with _____ (Tony and I).

Unscramble the sentences

1. ___ ___ ___ ___ ___ .
much / very / it / I / like

2. ___ ___ ___ ___ ___ .
every day / plays / them / with / she

3. ___ ___ ___ ___ ___ .
We / much / very / like / him

4. ___ ___ ___ ___ ___ .
every day / I / her / to / talk

5. ___ ___ ___ ___ ___ .
They / at school / me / to / talk

## How well did you do in this unit?
Write the CAN DO statement and assess yourself.
**Write 3, 2, or 1**
**3** = VERY WELL
**2** = WELL
**1** = NOT SO WELL

I CAN...
_____
_____
_____
_____
_____
_____
_____

**Level FOUR. Unit ELEVEN.**
Let's play with numbers!

## Learn the numbers up to 100

1 one
2 two
3 three
4 four
5 five

6 six
7 seven
8 eight
9 nine
10 ten

11 eleven
12 twelve
13 thirteen
14 fourteen
15 fifteen

16 sixteen
17 seventeen
18 eighteen
19 nineteen
20 twenty

30 thirty
40 forty
50 fifty
60 sixty
70 seventy
80 eighty
90 ninety
100 one hundred

Write the numbers

20 _____
30 _____
40 _____
50 _____
60 _____
70 _____
80 _____
90 _____

# 26.2 Dialogs

**Level FOUR. Unit ELEVEN.**
Let's play with numbers!

## Practice the dialogs

How many roses are there in the vase?
-Let me count them!
-There are twenty roses in the vase.
Ok, thank you.

How many children are there in the classroom?
-Let me count them!
-There are thirty children.
Ok, thank you

How many fish are there in the bowl?
-Let me count them!
-There are ten fish in the bowl.
Ok, thank you.

How many geese are there in the sky?
-Let me count them!
-There are fifty geese in the sky.
Ok, thank you!

How many matches are there in the box?
-Let me count them!
-There are eighty matches in the box.
Ok, thank you!

*Now you!*

How many _____ are there in the ____?
-Let me count them! There are ___ ____ in the ____.
Ok, thank you!

**Level FOUR. Unit ELEVEN.**
*Let's play with numbers!*

## Let's count!

Our class today is going to be about numbers- I love numbers! Miss Patty says that we have to count the objects in the pictures that she gives us. She says: "Let's count!" My pictures have children and buses. Let me count them; there are thirty children and sixty buses! Sandy has to count roses and geese; there are twenty roses and fifty geese! Tony has fish and matches. There are ten fish and eighty matches! It's Andy's turn; there are forty men and one hundred boxes in his pictures. WOW! We are counting all the way up to one hundred, that's a lot of numbers! Can you count up to one hundred? Let's count!

Circle the correct number

1. There are 20 roses.
   ten   twenty   thirty
2. There are 30 children.
   twenty   thirty   forty
3. There are 10 fish.
   forty   fifty   ten
4. There are 50 geese.
   fifty   sixty   forty
5. There are 40 men.
   twenty   thirty   forty
6. There are 80 matches.
   twenty   ten   eighty

Circle true or false

1. Sandy has to count roses and geese.
   True   False
2. Andy has to count fish and matches
   True   False
3. Tony has to count men and boxes.
   True   False
4. Lucy has to count buses and children.
   True   False

## 26.4 Writing

**Level FOUR. Unit ELEVEN.**
*Let's play with numbers!*

Choose a word and fill in a blank. You can use the numbers as many times as you wish. Then read aloud.

> Let's count!
> Our class today is going to be about numbers- I love numbers!
> Miss Patty says that we have to count
> what is in the pictures that she will give us.
> She says, "Let's count!"
> My pictures have children and buses. Let me count them;
> there are _____ children and _____ buses!
> Sandy has to count roses and geese;
> there are _____ roses and _____ geese!
> Tony has fish and matches.
> There are _____ fish and _____ matches! It's Andy's turn;
> there are _____ men and _____ boxes in his pictures.
> WOW! We are counting all the way up to one hundred,
> that's a lot of numbers!
> Can you count up to one hundred? Let's count!

> ten • twenty • thirty • forty • fifty
> sixty • seventy • eighty • ninety • one hundred

12    19    20    80

40    30

**Level FOUR. Unit ELEVEN.**
*Let's play with numbers!*

26.5 Language in use

**PLURAL FORM OF NOUNS**
We make most plural of nouns by adding "S"
book = books

We make plural of nouns that end in S, CH, SH, X or S by adding "ES"
match = matches
box = boxes

Write the plural form of the nouns.

1. box _____
2. brush _____
3. bus _____
4. dress _____
5. fox _____
6. gas _____
7. lunch _____
8. match _____
9. sandwich _____
10. wish _____

**Time to Rhyme!**

One, two,
Buckle my shoe;
Three, four,
Knock at the door;
Five, six,
Pick-up sticks;
Seven eight,
Lay them straight;
Nine, ten,
A big fat hen;
Eleven, twelve,
Dig and delve;
Thirteen, fourteen,
Maids a counting;
Fifteen, sixteen,
Maids in the kitchen;
Seventeen, eighteen,
Maids-a-waiting;
Nineteen, twenty,
My plate's empty.

## How well did you do in this unit?
Write the CAN DO statement and assess yourself.
**Write 3, 2, or 1**
**3** = VERY WELL
**2** = WELL
**1** = NOT SO WELL

I CAN...
_____
_____
_____
_____
_____
_____
_____

**Level FOUR. Unit TWELVE.**
*Let's play with opposites!*

## Learn the opposites

tall · short

thin · heavy

old · young

straight hair · curly hair

black hair · blonde hair

## 27.2 Dialogs

**Level FOUR. Unit TWELVE.**
Let's play with opposites!

Practice the dialogs

Is the teacher young or old?
-She is young.
Is the dentist young or old?
-He is old.

Is the farmer heavy or thin?
-He is thin.
Is the bus driver heavy or thin?
-He is heavy.

Is the pilot tall or short?
-He is tall.
Is the waiter tall or short?
-He is short.

Does the police officer have blonde or black hair?
-He has blonde hair.
Does the firefighter have blonde or black hair?
-She has black hair.

Does the doctor have curly or straight hair?
-She has curly hair.
Does the nurse have curly or straight hair?
-He has straight hair.

Does the _____ have ___ or ____ ____?
-She has ____

Level FOUR. Unit TWELVE.
Let's play with opposites!

27.3 Reading

## What do they look like?

There are many people that help us in our city; the doctor the nurse, the police officer and more. But what do they look like? Well, let's see, in my city…
The teacher is young and the dentist is old; they are so nice.
The farmer is thin and the bus driver is heavy; they are very reliable.
The pilot is tall and the waiter is short; they are very polite.
The police officer has blonde hair and the firefighter has black hair; they are so brave.
The doctor has curly hair and the nurse has straight hair; they are so caring.
I like them all; they all help us have a great city!

### Circle the correct option

1. The doctor has straight hair.
   True    False
2. The bus driver is heavy.
   True    False
3. The teacher is old.
   True    False
4. The farmer is heavy.
   True    False
5. The pilot is short.
   True    False
6. The nurse has straight hair.
   True    False
7. The firefighter has black hair.
   True    False

### Match the description with the community helpers

1. They are reliable.
2. They are nice.
3. They are polite.
4. They are brave.
5. They are caring.

(___) Doctor and nurse
(___) Farmer and bus driver
(___) Pilot and waiter
(___) Police officer and firefighter
(___) Teacher and dentist

## 27.4 Writing

**Level FOUR. Unit TWELVE.**
*Let's play with opposites!*

Choose a word and fill in a blank. You can use the adjectives as many times as you wish. Then read aloud.

---

**What do they look like?**

There are many people that help us in our city;
the doctor the nurse, the police officer and more.
But what do they look like? Well, let's see, in my city…
The teacher is ____ and the ____ is old; they are so nice.
The farmer is ____ and the bus driver is ____ ;
they are very reliable. The pilot is ____ and the waiter is ____ ;
they are very polite.
The police officer has ____ hair and the firefighter has ____ hair;
they are so brave.
The doctor has ____ hair and the nurse has ____ hair;
they are so caring.
I like them all; they all help us have a great city!

---

| tall   | short    |
|--------|----------|
| thin   | heavy    |
| old    | young    |
| curly  | straight |
| blonde | black    |

**Level FOUR. Unit TWELVE.**
*Let's play with opposites!*

We use adjectives to describe nouns.
We use the following adjectives
to describe physical appearance of people:
tall/short; thin/heavy; old/young;
curly hair/straight hair; blonde hair/black hair

We use the following adjectives to describe
the personality of people:
nice, reliable, polite, brave, caring

## Unscramble the sentences

1. ___ ___ ___ ___ .
   hair / curly / has / she
2. ___ ___ ___ ___ .
   he / hair / straight / has
3. ___ ___ ___ ___ .
   black / has / hair / she
4. ___ ___ ___ ___ .
   blonde / he / has / hair
5. ___ ___ ___ ___ .
   polite / is / the / waiter

## Match the opposite adjectives

blonde     black
curly     heavy
old     short
tall     straight
thin     young

## How well did you do in this unit?
Write the CAN DO statement and assess yourself.
**Write 3, 2, or 1**
**3** = VERY WELL
**2** = WELL
**1** = NOT SO WELL

I CAN...
_____
_____
_____
_____
_____
_____
_____

**Level FOUR. Unit THIRTEEN.**
*Let's play with time!*

**28.1** Vocabulary

Learn how to tell the time

What time is it?

It's 7:00 o'clock

It's 7:15
(quarter after seven)

It's 7:30
(half past seven)

It's 7:45
(quarter before eight)

It's 8:10
(ten after eight)

It's 8:40
(twenty before nine)

### 28.2 Dialogs

Level FOUR. Unit THIRTEEN.
Let's play with time!

## Practice the dialogs

Hurry up, please!
-Why? What time is it?
It's ten past seven. It's time to get up.
-OK, I'm ready.

Hurry up, please!
-Why? What time is it?
It's half past seven. It's time to go to school.
-OK, I'm ready.

Hurry up, please!
-Why? What time is it?
It's eight o'clock. It's time to start class!
-OK, I'm ready.

Hurry up, please!
-Why? What time is it?
It's quarter to ten. It's recess time.
-OK, I'm ready.

Hurry up, please!
-Why? What time is it?
It's two o'clock. It's time to go home.
-OK, I'm ready.

Now you!

Hurry up, please!
-Why? What time is it?
It's quarter past _____. It's time to go to the _____.
-OK, I'm ready.

**Level FOUR. Unit THIRTEEN.**
Let's play with time!

## My school day

My school day starts at the same time every day.
My mom wakes me up at seven o'clock.
I get up and try to get ready as fast as I can.
My dad takes me to school at half past seven.
My classes start at eight o'clock.
Miss Patty is always there with a big smile to welcome us.
We all come into the classroom and start our school day.
We also have special classes; music, computer and others.
They start at ten to nine.
Recess starts at quarter to ten. We have lunch and play during recess.
We all love recess. We go back to the classroom at quarter past ten.
We continue our classes and finally the school day is complete.
We can go home ten past two.
I am very happy when Miss Patty says: "Time to go home."
What time do you start your school day?

### Circle the correct option

1. What time do you get up?
   7:00    7:30    8:00
2. What time do you go to school?
   7:00    7:30    8:00
3. What time do you start class?
   7:00    7:30    8:00
4. What time do you have special classes?
   8:50    9:45    10:15
5. What time do you start recess?
   8:50    9:45    10:15
6. What time do you go back to the classroom?
   8:50    9:45    10:15

### Match the sentences with the correct times

1. Mom wakes me up at:    (___)
2. Dad takes me to school at:    (___)
3. Classes start at:    (___)
4. Special classes start at:    (___)
5. Recess is at:    (___)
6. We go back to the classroom at:    (___)
7. We can go home at:    (___)

a    b    c
d    e    g
     f

## 28.4 Writing

**Level FOUR. Unit THIRTEEN.**
Let's play with time!

Choose a word and fill in a blank. You can use the times as many times as you wish. Then read aloud.

### My school day

My school day starts at the same time every day.
My mom wakes me up at _____.
I get up and try to get ready as fast as I can.
My dad takes me to school at _____.
My classes start at eight o'clock.
Miss Patty is always there with a big smile to welcome us.
We all come into the classroom and start our school day.
We also have special classes; music, computer and others.
They start at _____. Recess starts at _____.
We have lunch and play during recess.
We all love recess. We go back to the classroom at _____.
We continue our classes and finally the school day is complete.
We can go home _____.
I am very happy when Miss Patty says: "Time to go home."
What time do you start your school day?

7:00 • 7:15 • 7:30 • 7:45 • 8:00 • 8:50 • 9:00
9:45 • 10:15 • 12:15 • 2:10

## Level FOUR. Unit THIRTEEN.
### Let's play with time!

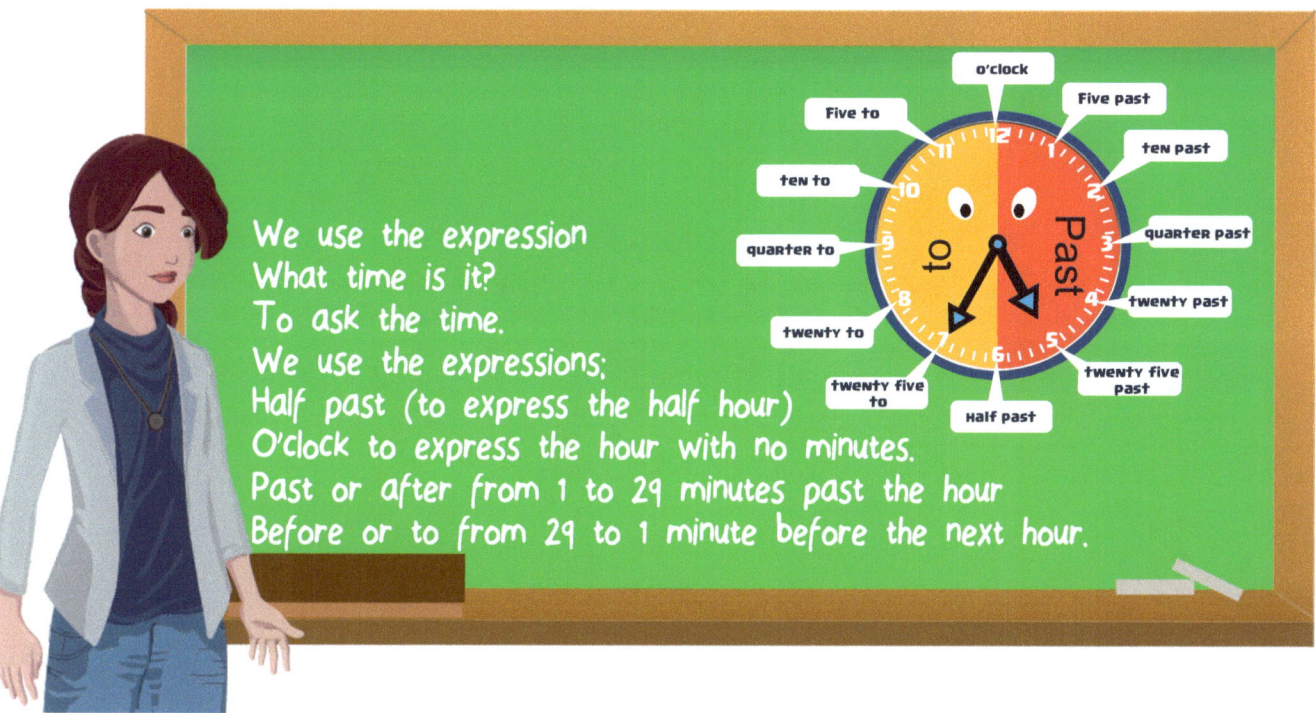

We use the expression
What time is it?
To ask the time.
We use the expressions:
Half past (to express the half hour)
O'clock to express the hour with no minutes.
Past or after from 1 to 29 minutes past the hour
Before or to from 29 to 1 minute before the next hour.

### Unscramble the sentences

1. ___ ___ ___ ___ .
   ten / past / half / it's
2. ___ ___ ___ ___ .
   It's / quarte / before / ten
3. ___ ___ ___ ___ .
   quarter / ten / after / it's
4. ___ ___ ___ .
   o'clock / eight / it's
5. ___ ___ ___ ___ .
   nine / past / twenty / it's
6. ___ ___ ___ ___ .
   eleven / it's / to / twenty

### Match the times

a) It's ten before nine
b) It's five o'clock
c) It's half past three
d) It's quarter after two
e) It's quarter before one
f) It's twenty after eight

5:00 (___)   8:50 (___)
2:15 (___)   3:30 (___)
8:20 (___)   12:45 (___)

## How well did you do in this unit?
Write the CAN DO statement and assess yourself.
**Write 3, 2, or 1**
**3** = VERY WELL
**2** = WELL
**1** = NOT SO WELL

I CAN...
_____
_____
_____
_____
_____
_____
_____

# Level FOUR. Unit FOURTEEN.
## Let's play with the days!

## Learn the days of the week

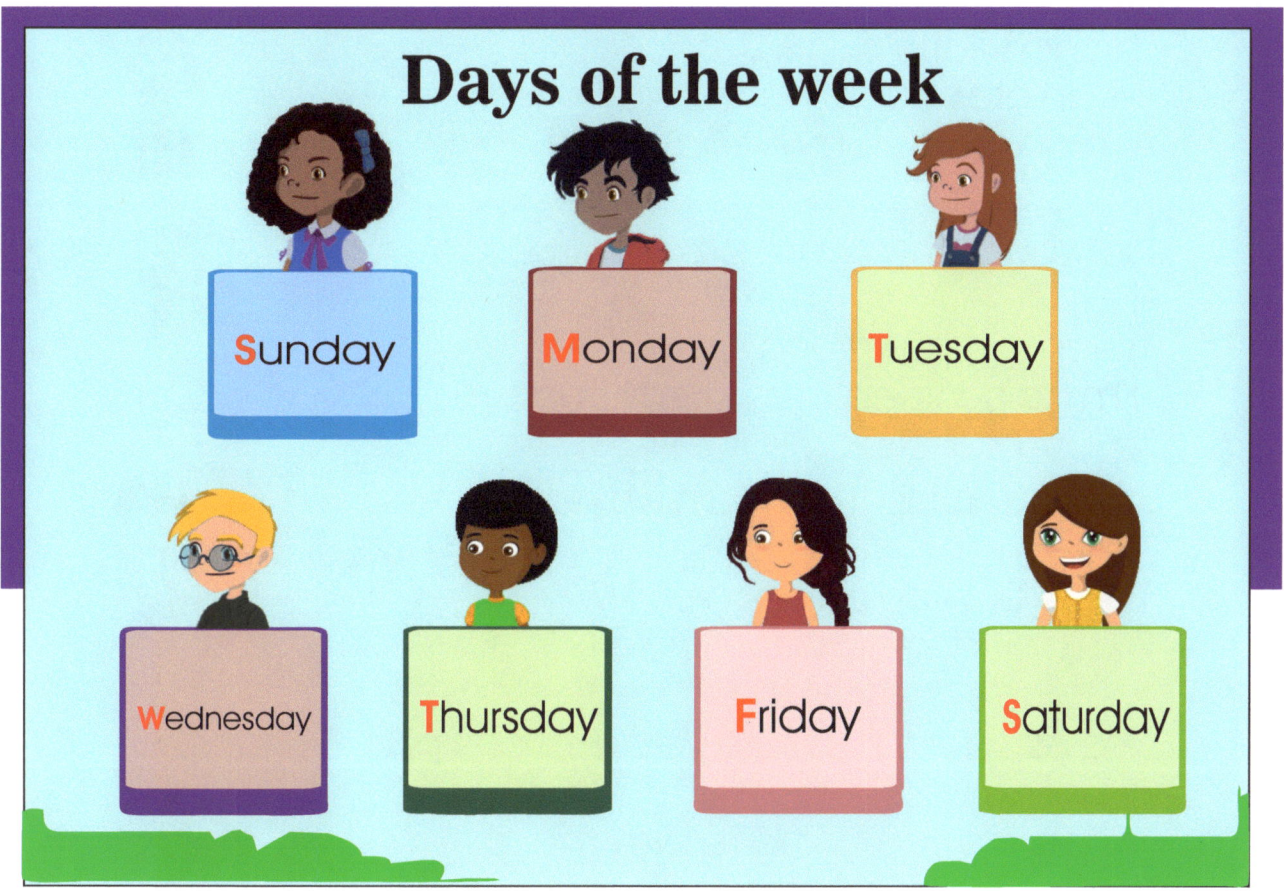

**Monday**

**Tuesday**   **Friday**

**Saturday**

**Wednesday**

**Sunday**

**Thursday**

| Y | A | D | S | R | U | H | T | W | Y |
|---|---|---|---|---|---|---|---|---|---|
| Y | U | F | O | Y | Y | E | E | F | A |
| C | A | B | R | A | B | D | G | N | D |
| P | F | D | D | I | N | U | B | V | S |
| I | G | N | R | E | D | M | C | B | E |
| X | U | F | S | U | D | A | P | L | U |
| S | D | D | Z | K | T | Z | Y | B | T |
| B | A | M | O | N | D | A | Y | A | B |
| Y | H | D | K | D | N | F | S | I | H |
| S | A | B | X | P | E | J | B | G | I |

## 29.2 Dialogs

**Level FOURTEEN.**
Let's play with the days!

### Practice the dialogs

Are you going to study on Sunday?
-No, I'm not.
When are you going to study?
-I'm going to study on Saturday.

Are you going to eat pizza on Tuesday?
-No, I'm not.
When are you going to eat pizza?
-I'm going to eat pizza on Monday.

Are you going to play on Monday?
-No, I'm not.
When are you going to play?
-I'm going to play on Sunday.

Are you going to play the guitar on Friday?
-No, I'm not.
When are you going to play the guitar?
-I'm going to play the guitar on Thursday.

Are you going to have a party on Saturday?
-No, I'm not.
When are you going to have a party?
-I'm going to have a party on Friday.

Now you!

Are you going to _____ on _____?
-No, I'm not.
When are you going to _____?
-I'm going to _____ on _____.

**Level FOUR. Unit FOURTEEN.**
*Let's play with the days!*

## What are you going to do this week?

My friends and I are going to be very busy this week.
What are we going to do? Well let's see!
Andy is going to study on Saturday.
He isn't going to study on Sunday.
Tony isn't going to play soccer on Monday.
He's going to play soccer on Sunday;
he isn't going to watch a movie on Wednesday
but he's going to watch a movie on Tuesday.
Lucy is going to eat pizza with her friends on Monday.
She isn't going to eat pizza on Tuesday;
and also she's going to practice tennis on Wednesday;
she isn't going to practice tennis on Thursday.
I am going to be very busy too.
I am going to play the guitar on Thursday;
I am not going to play the guitar on Friday
because I am going to have a party on Friday!
Do you want to come? What are going to do this week?

**Circle the correct option**

1. When is Sandy going to play the guitar?
   Friday   Thursday   Saturday
2. When is Sandy going to have a party?
   Friday   Thursday   Saturday
3. When is Andy going to study?
   Friday   Thursday   Saturday
4. When is Tony going to play soccer?
   Monday   Sunday   Wednesday
5. When is Tony going to watch a movie?
   Tuesday   Wednesday   Monday

**Circle ✓ if the sentence is true**
**Circle ✗ if the sentence is false**

1. Andy is going to study on Sunday.
   ✓   ✗
2. Tony is going to play soccer on Sunday.
   ✓   ✗
3. Lucy is going to eat pizza with her friends on Tuesday.
   ✓   ✗
4. Tony is going to watch a movie on Tuesday.
   ✓   ✗
5. Lucy is going to practice tennis on Thursday.
   ✓   ✗

## 29.4 Writing

**Unit TWENTY-NINE**
*Let's play with the days!*

Choose a word and fill in a blank. You can use the days of the week as many times as you wish. Then read aloud.

### What are you going to do this week?

My friends and I are going to be very busy this week.
What are we going to do? Well let's see!
Andy is going to study on _____.
He isn't going to study on _____.
Tony isn't going to play soccer on _____.
He's going to play soccer on _____;
he isn't going to watch a movie on _____
but he's going to watch a movie on _____.
Lucy is going to eat pizza with her friends on _____.
She isn't going to eat pizza on _____;
and also she's going to practice tennis on _____;
she isn't going to practice tennis on _____.
I am going to be very busy too.
I am going to play the guitar on _____;
I am not going to play the guitar on _____ because
I am going to have a party on _____!
Do you want to come? What are going to do this week?

Sunday· Monday · Tuesday · Wednesday ·
Thursday · Friday · Saturday

**Level FOUR. Unit FOURTEEN.**
*Let's play with the days!*

### Review of Future Tense
BE + going to + verb
We use it to make a prediction especially if we have evidence and to express planned actions in the future.

**Affirmative**
Subject + BE + going to + verb + complement

**Negative**
Subject + BE + NOT + going to + verb + complement

**Interrogative**
BE + Subject + going to + verb + complement?

**Wh- questions**
WH + BE + subject + going to + verb + complement

### Unscramble the sentences

1. ____ ____ ____ ____ ____ .
Lucy / going to / is / eat pizza / on Tuesday

2. ____ ____ ____ ____ ____ .
on Thursday / Sandy / going to / is / play the guitar

3. ____ ____ ____ ____ ____ .
on Friday / is / going to / Tony / watch a movie

4. ____ ____ ____ ____ ____ .
Andy / on Sunday / is / going to / study

### Which day comes next?

1. Tuesday, Wednesday, Thursday
   _____
2. Monday, Tuesday, Wednesday
   _____
3. Friday, Saturday, Sunday
   _____
4. Saturday, Sunday, Monday
   _____
5. Thursday, Friday, Saturday
   _____
6. Sunday, Monday, Tuesday
   _____

Monday · Tuesday · Wednesday
Thursday · Friday · Saturday
Sunday

# How well did you do in this unit?
Write the CAN DO statement and assess yourself.
**Write 3, 2, or 1**
**3** = VERY WELL
**2** = WELL
**1** = NOT SO WELL

I CAN...
_____
_____
_____
_____
_____
_____
_____

**Level FOUR. Unit FIFTEEN.**
*Let's play with the months of the year!*

Learn the months of the year

## Months of the year

### Calendar

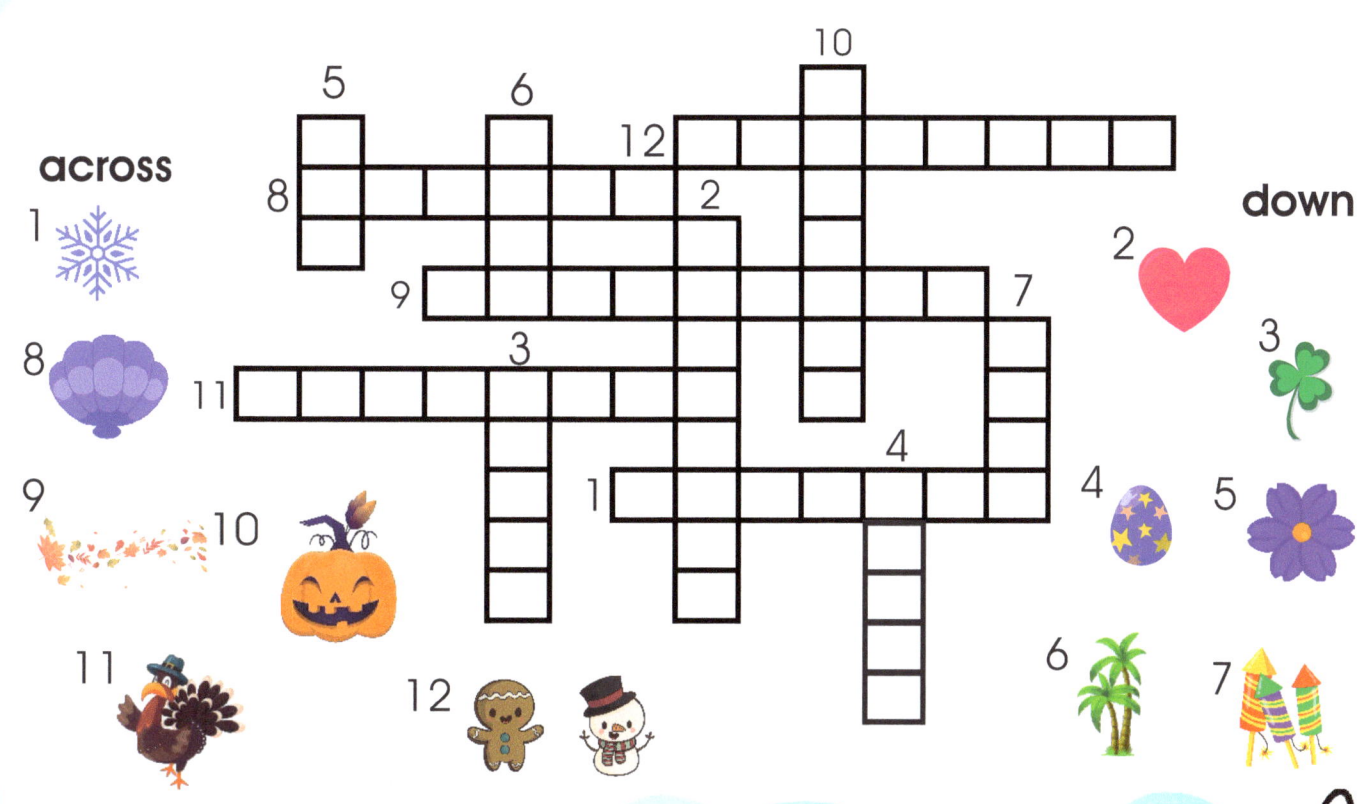

## 30.2 Dialogs

**Level FOUR. Unit FIFTEEN.**
Let's play with the months of the year!

### Practice the dialogs

Will you go skiing in January?
-No, I won't.
When will you go skiing?
-I will go skiing in February.

Will you run in the marathon in May?
-No, I won't.
When will you run in the marathon?
-I will run in the marathon in June.

Will you swim in the pool in July?
-No, I won't.
When will you swim in the pool?
-I will swim in the pool in August.

Will you go on vacation in March?
-No, I won't.
When will you go on vacation?
-I will go on vacation in April.

Will you participate in the play in November?
-No, I won't.
When will you participate in the play?
-I will participate in the play in December.

*Now you!*

Will you _____ in _____?
-No, I won't.
When will you _____?
-I will _____ in _____.

**Level FOUR. Unit FIFTEEN.**
*Let's play with the months of the year!*

## What will you do next year?

Next year will be very busy for all my friends.
What will they do? Let's see…
Andy will go skiing in February;
he won't go skiing in January.
Lucy will go on vacation in April;
she won't go on vacation in March.
Tony will run in the marathon in June; he won't run in May.
Harry will swim in the pool in August; he won't swim in July.
Tom will march in the parade in October;
he won't march in September.
Michelle will participate in the play in the December;
she won't participate in November.
Certainly all my friends are going to be very busy all year long.
What will you do next year? Will you be busy?

**Answer the questions**

1. When will Andy go skiing?
   _____
2. When will Lucy go on vacation?
   _____
3. When will Tony run in a marathon?
   _____
4. When will Harry swim in the pool?
   _____
5. When will Tom march in the parade?
   _____

Circle ✓ if the sentence is true
Circle ✗ if the sentence is false

1. Andy will go skiing in February.
   ✓   ✗
2. Lucy will go on vacation in May.
   ✓   ✗
3. Tony will run in a marathon in June.
   ✓   ✗
4. Harry will swim in the pool in August.
   ✓   ✗
5. Tom will march in the parade in September.
   ✓   ✗

### 30.4 Writing

**Level FOUR. Unit FIFTEEN.**
*Let's play with the months of the year!*

Choose a word and fill in a blank. You can use the months of the year as many times as you wish. Then read aloud.

What will you do next year?

Next year will be very busy for all my friends.
What will they do? Let's see…
Andy will go skiing in _____;
he won't go skiing in _____.
Lucy will go on vacation in _____;
she won't go on vacation in _____.
Tony will run in the marathon in _____;
he won't run in _____.
Harry will swim in the pool in _____;
he won't swim in _____.
Tom will march in the parade in _____;
he won't march in _____.
Michelle will participate in the play in the _____;
she won't participate in _____.
Certainly all my friends will be very busy all year long.
What will you do next year? Will you be busy?

January · February · March · April · May
June · July · August · September
October · November · December

**Level FOUR. Unit FIFTEEN.**
*Let's play with the months of the year!*

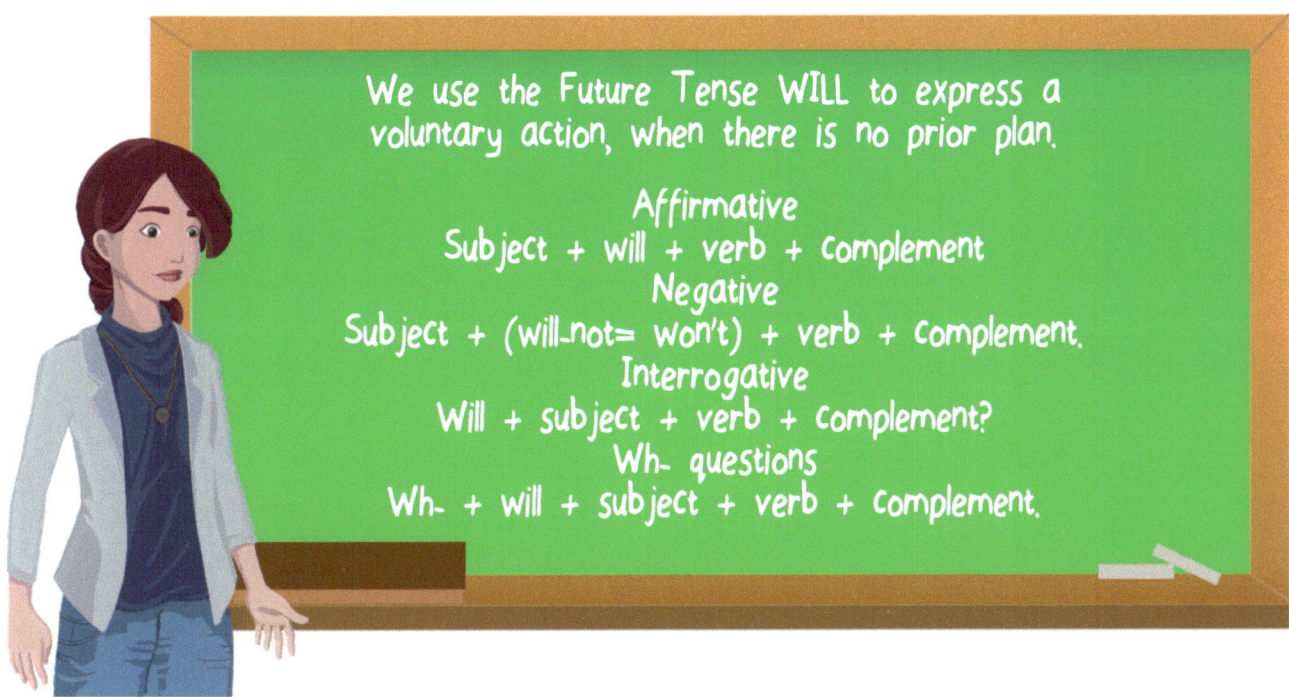

We use the Future Tense WILL to express a voluntary action, when there is no prior plan.

**Affirmative**
Subject + will + verb + complement
**Negative**
Subject + (will not = won't) + verb + complement.
**Interrogative**
Will + subject + verb + complement?
**Wh- questions**
Wh- + will + subject + verb + complement.

## Unscramble the sentences

1. _____ _____ _____ _____ ?
   in February / will / Andy go skiing

2. _____ _____ _____ _____ .
   Lucy / won't / go on vacation / in May

3. _____ _____ _____ _____ .
   run in a marathon / will Tony / in June

4. _____ _____ _____ _____ ?
   in august / Sandy swim in the pool / will

## Find the months of the year

| H | N | F | T | P | J | L | A | R | D |
|---|---|---|---|---|---|---|---|---|---|
| C | M | O | Y | S | I | U | E | P | E |
| R | A | Q | V | R | U | B | L | J | C |
| A | Y | G | P | E | M | G | A | Y | E |
| M | A | A | F | E | M | N | U | U | M |
| D | S | I | T | Y | U | B | J | A | B |
| F | R | P | T | A | Q | S | E | N | E |
| F | E | B | R | U | A | R | Y | R | R |
| S | H | Y | R | E | B | O | T | C | O |
| F | P | X | B | D | K | J | U | N | E |

JANUARY • FEBRUARY • MARCH
APRIL • MAY • JUNE
JULY • AUGUST • SEPTEMBER
OCTOBER • NOVEMBER • DECEMBER

# How well did you do in this unit?
Write the CAN DO statement and assess yourself.
**Write 3, 2, or 1**
**3** = VERY WELL
**2** = WELL
**1** = NOT SO WELL

I CAN...
_____
_____
_____
_____
_____
_____
_____

# REFERENCES

- Communicative Language Learning. Retrieved August 23, 2019 from:
  http://www.educationbridge-id.com/news-a-article/72-communicative-language-teaching-clt.html

- Brown, H. Douglas (1994). Principles of Language Learning and Teaching. Prentice Hall.

- Beale, Jason (2008). Is communicative language teaching a thing of the past?. TESOL article.

- Harmer, Jeremy (2007). How to teach English. Pearson Longman.

- Richards, Jack C (2002). Methodology in Language Teaching. Cambridge University Press.

- Willis, Jane (1996). A Framework for Task-Based Learning. Longman.

- Hermitt, A. (2015). Spiral Learning, a superior approach? *In Families.com*. Retrieved January 9th, 2015, from http://www.families.com/blog/spiral-learning-a-superior approach.

- Fleming, N. Baume, D. (2006) Learning Styles.

- Again: VARKing up the right tree!, Educational Developments, SEDA Ltd, Issue 7.4 Nov. 2006.

- Harmer, Jeremy. How to *Teach English.* Harlow: Longman, 1998. Krashen, Stephen D., and Terrell, Tracy D. The *Natural Approach.* Oxford: Pergamon, 1983.

- Sökmen, Anita J. "Current Trends in Teaching Second Language Vocabulary". *In Vocabulary: Description, Acquisition and Pedagogy,* edited by N. Schmitt and M. McCarthy, 237-257 England: Cambridge University Press, 1997.

- Snow, Marguerite Ann. *"Teaching English as a Second or Foreign Language".* In Content-Based and Immersion Models for Second and Foreign Language Teaching" Edited by M. Celce-Murcia. Heinle & Heinle Thomson Learning, 2001.

- Roth, Genevieve. *Teaching Very Young Children.* Richmond Handbooks for English Teachers. London: Richmond Publishing. 1998.

- freepik.com (website). This website is operated by Freepik Company, S.L., registered in the Commercial Registry of Málaga, volume 4994, sheet 217, page number MA-113059, with Tax Number B-93183366 and registered office at 13 Molina Lario St., 5th floor, 29015, Málaga, Spain ("Company"). All intellectual property rights over the Website, the Services, and/or the Freepik Content, its design, and source code, and all content included in any of them (including without limitation text, images, animations, databases, graphics, logos, trademarks, icons, buttons, pictures, videos, sound recordings, etc.) belong or are licensed to the Company.

# ABOUT THE AUTHOR

Patricia Avila has been an English teacher for more than 45 years in her native Tijuana, B. C. She has a Bachelor's in Education from the National Pedagogical University (UPN).

Her experience as a teacher ranges from Kindergarten to Masters. She has functioned as coordinator of Bachelor's in ESL Teaching, as well as for various other universities; she has also worked as an Academic Consultant for different Publishing Houses for more than 15 years. Her wide experience and love for young learners has given her the opportunity to share with you SMART DOLPHIN ZONE, a series that will enhance the learning of English in a **dynamic** and **fun** way.

**METHODOLOGIES:**
- Vocabulary learning
- Communicative Language Learning
- Integrated Skills Approach
- Spiral Learning
- Topic Based Approach

**FEATURES:**
- Each book with 30 units
- Two different levels in each book
- Each unit has five lessons:

    Lesson 1: Vocabulary
    Lesson 2: Dialogs
    Lesson 3: Reading
    Lesson 4: Writing
    Lesson 5: Language in Use

- **Special features:**

    Songs, rhymes, jokes for kids, advertisements, classical stories, fables, movie reviews, short biographies, short classical stories, story fragments and weather forecasts.

Interested in purchasing a platform that is the perfect match for this book?
Email us: books@unilxeducation.com

www.ingramcontent.com/pod-product-compliance
Lightning Source LLC
Chambersburg PA
CBHW041513220426
43668CB00002B/15